LITTLE IRELAND

Memories of a Cleator childhood

SEAN CLOSE

Produced by
Questa Publishing, Preston

Printed by
Printexpress (Cumbria) Limited, Whitehaven

Close Publishing

© Sean Close, 2001
ISBN 0-9540673-0-4

No part of this book may be reproduced, stored in a retrieval system or transmitted in any form or by any means without the prior permission in writing of the publisher.

CONTENTS

Dedication 6
Acknowledgements 6
Preface 7
Prospect Row (circa 1958) 8

1	Cleator before the invasion	9
2	Father McCann and the Priory Club	13
3	Rory Quiggley	19
4	My sister Margaret	22
5	The Church	29
6	Old Crado does his worst	34
7	Miss Cairns	37
8	Nancy with the laughing eyes	42
9	The Missioners	44
10	The Legion of Mary	47
11	The Young Men's Society	51
12	The Sacred Mysteries	52
13	Keir Hardie Avenue	55
14	Birks Road - Renato Segalini	64
15	Yellow Jaundice	74
16	Red Hill Quarry	81
17	The Black Ship	82
18	The Lucky Road	86
19	Crab Fair	90
20	Recurring Dreams	93
21	Workington Infirmary	97
22	The Attic Stairs	100
23	Miles Bowden	106
24	That Touchy Thing	108
25	A Rafting Experience	109
26	Eccentrics	113
27	Street Life	117
28	The Banshee	118
29	The month of May	120
30	The 11+ and extra curricular activities	122
31	I'm in love	125
32	Bricey Finn	127
33	Linda Strickland	129
34	Escape from Auschwitz	135
35	F****** John	138
36	The Old Silver Rover	141

DEDICATION

I would like to dedicate this book to my parents Jay and Eileen Close who gave me my childhood, allowed me the space to develop as an individual and let me go when I was ready to face the world on my own. Their parental skills were instinctive and soundly based. They are what made me the man I am today.

ACKNOWLEDGEMENTS

I have received many good will messages and encouragement during the writing of this book for which I am most grateful.

I would like to thank the following people: Ruth Close my wee daughter; Rachael Close my other wee daughter; Margaret Delin my wee sister; Jean Law; Sheila Mitchell; Ann Nattrass; Fr. Tim Sullivan (St. Mary's, Cleator); Christine Peacock (Whitehaven News); my family past and present; the people of Cleator and Cleator Moor, who provided me with the colourful characters I have written about.

And last but not least, my wee wife Joan who sacrificed our quality time together to allow me to indulge myself in writing this book and for her constant encouragement and help.

With out these people my *Little Ireland* recollections would not have been possible.

Thank you all.

Sean Close, May 2001

PREFACE

The post war years of my childhood, in the 1950s, were a wonderful time to grow up in. God was in his heaven and the world seemed at peace. People talked about 'Peace in our time' and there was a feeling of hope. I was born into a large extended family of four children and more aunties, uncles and cousins than you could shake a stick at.

I know it can be easy to see memories through rose-coloured glasses, but my childhood really was rose coloured. The little village of Cleator in the 1950s with its soft-sandstone terraced houses was surrounded by fresh countryside on three sides and the gentle slopes of Dent Mountain on the fourth. It was intersected by numerous becks, and on the banks of the majestic River Ehen, or Hen Beck as we called it, life was set at a very gentle pace - and the onset of television wasn't even thought of. Perhaps that sounds like a very romantic notion, but it's how it seemed to me at the time of thinking.

People were nest building after the terrible war years; taking stock and looking forward to what suddenly seemed like a real future. Calder Hall, the atomic energy plant not known yet as Sellafield, was being built and there was full employment. The feeling of camaraderie and neighbourliness, which the war instilled, was still prevalent. Children could roam the fields and fell sides in absolute safety. Child molesting was unknown and senior citizens were treated with respect.

How glorious to be a child in such times!

Now, as a middle-aged man, with my children grown up and, sadly, both my parents dead, I often find my mind wandering back to my childhood days and reflecting on how different childhood seems to be today. So, I decided to write down some of my memories so that my children and grandchildren - and anyone else who cares to read these pages - may have some sort of insight into what now seems like a bygone age.

Please drift back with me to the days when boys wore short trousers until they were eleven or twelve, and girls never wore trousers.

LITTLE IRELAND

Prospect Row, circa 1958

	SURNAME	ADULTS	CHILDREN
1.	BOHAN	Mrs Calvert (Gran), Tommy & Mary Bohan	Ada, Sonia, Tommy & Margaret
2.	STANBOROUGH	Nathan & Maggie	Ronnie, Kenneth, John & Marian
3.	ROONEY	Elsie, Alice, Hannah & another sister sometimes	Joe, Christine, twin & Alan
4.	McCARTEN	Esther & sister	
5.	LAWSON	Sarah (widow)	Joe, Veronica, Frances, Jim, Sally, Mary & Peter
6.	KEWLEY	Mr & Mrs	Grandparents of Stanboroughs
7.	TOLSEN	George & Mary	George, Joan, Nicholas, another daughter & Billy
8.	PALMER	Ike & Ethel	Jackie, Richard, Lillian, Lesley, Albert, Trevor & Wren
9.	WOODS	Mr & Mrs (Annie)	Ina, Stan, Jim & 1 much younger son (suicide, Cleator Moor
10.	DAVIDSON	Mr & Mrs (Mary) (formerly Yankowski. Changed name by Deed Poll)	Dorothy, Cecilia, Alex & June
11.	SMITH	Frank & Lizzie	Doreen, Betty & Frankie
12.	STONES	Tommy and Annie	Barbara, Mary, Tommy, Billy and Tony
13.	FLEMING	Katie (spinster)	Later Margaret Fleming - niece (29 Prospect) married - Mr & Mrs Park
14.	MALAGHAN	Walter & Joan	Ian & Joy
15.	BYRNES	Mrs & Mary (daughter)	Later Eileen Morton & husband (grand-daughter)
16.	GRAHAM	Mrs (widow)	Mike, Eunie, later Mike & family
17.	STEWART	Kathleen	Sadie & Cathy
18.	DAWSON	Frank & Minnie	Gerard & Jenny
19.	FOWLER	George & Belle	Peggy, Anne & Peter
20.	DEVOY	Eddie & Winnie	Maureen, Sean & Jimmy
21.	MAGEE	Alice	Widow - grown up family away
22.	WHITE	Georgina (spinster) & George (brother)	Margaret, Ronnie, Joan & possibly another older brother
23.	EILBECK	Mrs (Mumma) - later Mr and Mrs Kelly	Veronica (daughter) & Peter Stewart (later Billy & Annie)
24.	HERALD	Edward & Mary	Maureen, Louie, Eddie, Carole & Anne
25.	TALLON	John & Mary	Sadie, Nellie, Josie, Tess & John (died just before 5th birthday)
26.	DAWSON	John & Annie	Sheila, Janet, Pamela, Marjorie & Jane
27.	McATEER	John & Katie	Anne & Rosalyn
28.	WOODS	Geordie & Maggie	Terry Youdale (grandson)
29.	MORGAN	Martha (spinster)	Maureen (niece) married Richard Carr and lived there for a while
30.	FLEMING	Jack & Emily	Margaret, Joan, John, Teddy, Vincent & Eileen
31.	CLOSE	Jay & Eileen	Barry, Sean, Stephen & Margaret
32.	FARRAN	Bert & Evelyn	Isabelle, Joe, Wendy & Catherine
33.	McCOURT	Barnie & Nellie	Julia & Eileen (other children married)

1
CLEATOR BEFORE THE INVASION

Cleator had been a farming area before the middle of the nineteenth century. Mainly small farms of no more than thirty to forty acres, with the exception of three large landowners - the Ainsworths, Lindows and the Lowthers - who owned practically two-thirds of the good arable land. They had tenant farmers on their farms and got rich off the backs of those hard-working people.

The landowners had interests apart from farming of course, and were involved in the spice and rum trades from Africa and Jamaica, and the new real-growth industry, the hematite and iron ore mines. The slave trade touched our local shores at Whitehaven for a short time, but the real surge of populous to our little village came with the migration of Irish settlers escaping from the potato famine in Ireland from 1845 to 1848 (three short years of absolute devastation). My ancestors were forced to leave the Emerald Isle in search of a new life in what they expected would be Utopia. They were joined by Manx, Cornishmen and men from the shires. All desperate for work in the mines.

As far as I know from my research, very little has been written about those years immediately following the influx of the first Irish settlers, other than the factual information about it coinciding with the Industrial Revolution. Masses of people were required for the new coal and iron-ore mines opened in and around West Cumberland, and for the foundries and residual businesses that would be needed to support these industries. So my guess is the Irish settlers and others would be viewed with very mixed feelings by the small indigenous Anglo-Saxon population, because, after all, they were two very different cultures.

The population grew from 750 in 1840 to 3,000 in 1850 and within a generation had risen to 10,000 resulting in the new town of Cleator Moor.

Imagine, if you can, the farming and rurally orientated occupations of the locals, the very slow and staid way of life they must have lived, and the routine rituals of everyday life - a lifestyle that had evolved over centuries. A high proportion of the population was staunch Church of England farming stock, with the rest of the population

LITTLE IRELAND

Methodists and Non-Conformist Christian groups. Everyone in this era had a strong Christian commitment. The simplistic way of life lent itself very nicely to the Christian ethos.

Then came the Catholics.

To glean some sort of insight into the nature, and culture of the Cleator Moor Irish psyche and its impact on the locality would require an in-depth study of Irish history. Too heavy for these pages, but certainly the circumstances of their arrival on English shores would have been from necessity not from choice. They wouldn't have been like most of the 1.5 million people who left Ireland in the mid-to-late nineteenth century. Most of whom were going to lands far away, like America and Australia, where they would embrace the challenge of a new country and be given equal rights with everyone else. The Cleator Moor Irish would see it more as moving nearer to their oppressors.

During the mid-to-late nineteenth century the English landlords, who owned huge estates in Ireland, were encouraging their tenant farmers to leave their small rented farms. Some were starving them out and some were paying their passage overseas. This was allowing them to carry out intensive farming for greater profits. This would be the main reason for the immigrants' arrival in Cleator Moor.

How far back do we need to go to trace our true roots? After all, if you believe Spanish historians, who claim the principal colonisers of Ireland way back in 700BC were Phoenicians, who settled in Ireland after roaming the world's oceans, then I should be looking to Spain for my ancestors. These Phoenician people were believed to be descendants of a tribe of Egyptians who were banished from Egypt at the time of Moses and who wandered through Africa for forty-four years and came by sea to the Pillars of Hercules, and through the Tuscan Sea to Spain.

I could go on *ad infinitum,* but for now I'll settle for my known links with Ireland and romanticise about those.

My maternal forebears and some of my paternal forebears would surely have come from the area around and to the east of Dublin, around the Wicklow Mountains, an area not unlike the Western Lakes near Cleator Moor. With names like Toole, Keough, Heron and McCumiskey (all Catholics) my father's forebears would hail from Northern Ireland: 'Close' is a Scottish or Northern Irish Protestant name. That in itself says something about them, because Catholic and

LITTLE IRELAND

Protestants in Ireland at the time were forbidden by law to marry. I can only speculate on the circumstances of their union.

My grandparents, and that is as far as I can go back in my memory, were second-generation Irish immigrants - 'As Irish as the pigs in Dublin.' To the unsuspecting Methodists, to hear them using expressions like, 'Mother of God, what will the Father think?' they must have seemed like blasphemous hooligans. For them it was 'life in the fast lane', to use a modern euphemism, because they had to make their mark in a land where to be a Catholic meant you were disadvantaged and discriminated against.

I don't want this book to degenerate into a political platform for the IRA or anything like it, but to get an insight into life at Cleator and the newly built town of Cleator Moor at this time it is necessary to understand the differences between these two factions.

The Irish incomers were not allowed to take office in any local government departments or to play any political roles at all. In fact, for a while they didn't even have the vote in local or national elections.

This was a very big disadvantage, because the incomers could not get proper representation. So, the mine owners were able to exploit them and build insubstantial housing with no proper infrastructure to support the by now very large group of people. The Irish were in the main, much louder and more boisterous and flamboyant than the Protestant families, and maybe liked a bit more to drink than they should have. They were a different kind of *hoi polloi,* and some inverted snobbery would be practised resulting in the Protestant population not wanting any of their daughters mixed up with the 'Catholic louts', and the Catholic populations not wanting any of their sons mixed up with that 'miserable Protestant lot'.

This is a huge generalisation, but indicates the sort of problems that were bound to occur. Not least because of the obvious differences in religious beliefs between the new, fast-becoming rival factions. So, to keep the peace, Catholics mixed with Catholics, and Protestants mixed with Protestants. It was not until my generation that the two were really integrated.

My father once told me that his father was one of eight children, half of whom were Catholic and half Protestant. Quite how the decision of who was nominated to which denomination was taken has disappeared in the annals of time. The logistics of half of the

LITTLE IRELAND

children attending Lamplugh Church of England School and half attending St Joseph's Roman Catholic School at Frizington must have been a mind-blowing experience for my great-grandmother. This must have at least had the positive effect of teaching the children some religious tolerance, I would have thought, although I saw little evidence of it in my father's Catholic family.

They lived in the small hamlet of Salter, consisting of two rows of sandstone miners' cottages, all demolished in the late 1950s. My great-grandfather worked in local mines around Lamplugh. When these pits were worked out, he and many other miners walked to and from Beckermet and Moresby pits every day, some ten to fifteen miles each way. They had a very hard existence, having only one day a week off work, Sunday. When the family finally moved to Cleator village, probably around the turn of the century, the men would obtain good, regular and sustained work in the immediate vicinity of Cleator and Cleator Moor. This was the boom time for the local mines and for West Cumberland in general.

This new form of prosperity was to be short-lived, and would exist only until the outbreak of World War I. Nothing could have prepared them for that, or the terrible Depression which followed during the 1920s and early 1930s. They had fallen from the frying pan into the fire in two generations.

By now their 'Englishness' must have been establishing itself in some way, but their Irish traditions and cultural idiosyncrasies were held onto, kept alive by their sheer numbers.

Prosperity eluded Cleator and Cleator Moor people between the wars, and to many men of my father's generation the Second World War was a happy release from poverty and unemployment. The war heralded the end of many of the religious and cultural differences between the Protestants and Catholics of Cleator Moor. With the odd exception, by my generation the two factions were quite well integrated.

By the time I was a lad in the 1950s and early 1960s Father McCann, the parish priest of Cleator, was a councillor for Ennerdale Rural District Council and on the Housing Committee. So, it could be said, at last the Catholics were well and truly represented.

2
FATHER McCANN

Father McCann was a very rotund and very jolly monk, not trained as a secular priest, but to spend a life of self-denial in the monasteries of Douai Abbey, the headquarters of the Benedictine Order in Berkshire. He must have thought that he had died and gone to Heaven already when he was sent to St Mary's, Cleator, or 'Little Ireland' as it was known locally, where he was loved and respected by all sections of society.

He lived in the parish for thirty-five years, so he earned his stripes.

In those days, processions were held where the faithful walked from Cleator Moor market place to the grotto at Cleator Catholic Church, a copy of the shrine to Our Lady of Lourdes in France, where in 1858 St Bernadette had apparitions of the Blessed Virgin Mary, who told her 'I am the Immaculate Conception'.

The grotto at Cleator is an exact copy of the grotto in Lourdes, and as such was a very popular place of pilgrimage for the Catholics from all over the North of England. An actual rock from the grotto at Lourdes was placed into the rocks at Cleator grotto, and remains there to this day. The grotto was built by out-of-work miners during the Depression in the 1920s and instigated by Father McCann's predecessor, the venerated Father Clayton, a saintly man, who gave the workers food parcels in return for their labour. By the time I was a lad in the '50s the place had become well established and indeed so too had the magnificent trees planted by the men some thirty years before.

The Priory Club

Just between the presbytery and St Mary's School was a semi-derelict property attached on the one side by the school and on the other by the Keenan's house, originally the priest-house belonging to the old church and now replaced by the new presbytery. These rooms had been neglected for many years and although not exactly derelict, were in a state of disrepair.

We decided it would make a great youth club, but first we would have to persuade Father McCann.

Now when I say we, I mean Stephen my brother, Paul Dunn, Wilfy

LITTLE IRELAND

Rogers, Raymond my cousin, Margaret Monaghan, my cousin Joan Fitzpatrick and Rory Quiggley. I was elected spokesperson because I had known Father McCann for years, and had served Mass for him and numerous other priests since I was just big enough to see over the alter rails.

I also had a persuasive nature, they all said.

But my skills were to be tested to their limits if I was to persuade Father McCann to let us use these otherwise forgotten premises for our brainchild. To be in charge of our own youth club, we'd love it.

Father McCann was no fool, he knew repairs would be necessary and money would need to be spent and he was fully committed financially and otherwise to his parishioners, the Bishop and Douai Abbey.

It couldn't be done.

After consultation with the newly-formed committee, Father McCann had to be re-approached this time with volunteers; people to do repairs and make safe the building. He agreed, on one condition - no fires were to be lit in the club under any circumstances. This was agreed and the Priory Club was born.

The repairs were done, a few floorboards replaced, windows made safe and a new lock put on the door. Father McCann came round to inspect. Unfortunately, he couldn't squeeze through the abnormally small front door of our new clubroom, let alone climb the narrow staircase. He was, as I said, rather portly.

He was quite happy though and re-affirmed his condition, 'No fires'. Well, if he hadn't mentioned a fire, we would never even have thought of it, but he had sown the seeds for us.

The room had just a skylight, an old cast-iron thing with yellow glass in it, so the funnel of our 'Heath Robinson' brazier-type fire fitted neatly through it. It was made from a large metal dustbin with holes poked into the bottom section of it and stood on building bricks. A hole was cut into the centre of the lid in which to insert a piece of asbestos drainpipe to be used as a chimney.

It worked a treat.

Each of us borrowed paper and some sticks and a few handfuls of coal from our parents' coal bins. There was a bit of smoke, but if you looked really hard you could almost make out figures standing a couple of feet away, so it was quite acceptable. Once the coal caught

LITTLE IRELAND

and the fire was roaring you could practically see to the other side of the room.

Facilities were basic: one electric light and no plug sockets, so for music we had to do with Joan Fitzpatrick's transistor radio. We could pick up Radio Luxembourg, and we had a record hop every Friday night. We bought a box of crisps from Mrs Murray's (just plain) and a couple of crates of lemonade from the Dent. It went swingingly for about three months or so - Freddie and the Dreamers, The Beatles, Chubby Checker, 'Let's Twist Again'.....we had the lot.

Father McCann would come occasionally to the bottom of the stairs, stand sideways and almost get through the door but never actually succeeded, and shout, 'Is everything alright, Sean?' and I'd hope he couldn't hear the crackling of the fire, and shout down, 'Yes Father, thank you.'

The entrance to the building was through a passageway. Part of the landing was above it and it was about four yards long. Immediately in front of you at the end of the passage were the toilets used by the parishioners to and from the grotto and church. They left a lot to be desired (the toilets, I mean!). To the right was a small yard and the entrance to the clubroom; to the left was a walled quadrangle with a gate leading into it. It was in fact the garden of the old churchhouse occupied by the Keenan family. It had an old-fashioned, romantic sort of feel about it; you could have been in Tuscany or Sorrento. The terracotta-coloured walls, the pots of deep red geraniums, and the hot bursts of sun filling the quadrangle in its exceptionally sheltered position made it feel quite foreign. The doorway of the club was for some reason only about two feet wide, and it led to a staircase of diminutive proportions. It could have been designed for Snow White and the Seven Dwarfs, so for our purposes it was fine.

There was a landing of about twenty feet and a window looking out onto the yard and the blank wall and roof of the school. An L-shaped room with a low ceiling was at the end of the landing with only a skylight for ventilation and light. It was small, but the excitement of having our own youth club was tremendous.

Now we needed to furnish it.

Bonfire Night was about three weeks away and Lenny Kiggins from Brookside had promised an old settee and a chair for the bonfire. Well that would be a start. Two very old church benches were already in the room, and the odd table and plenty of candles would

LITTLE IRELAND

be sufficient. Rory Quiggley came up trumps, he brought two conservatory tables from Larty's hut, and we were in business.

Lenny Kiggins was not quite ready to part with his furniture when we arrived to relieve him of it, mainly because he was still using it. Reluctantly, he chased one of the kids off the chair in the living room, who got off with a very bad grace because he'd been asleep. And then we were taken back into the front parlour to retrieve the settee.

The settee was a musty, donkey-brown moquette-covered thing, pre-war, and long overdue a good bonfiring. Clothes were piled up on it, and a peculiar lump was visible in the middle of it. It turned out to be a dog, a black and white mongrel, quite dead. Lenny was a little taken aback, but didn't seem to be upset, he said, 'I thought I hadn't seen that bloody thing for a week or so'.

I never felt quite right about that settee, and only sat on it when there was nowhere else to sit.

The Ghost of St Mary's had long been a well-known legend, but no sightings of it had been reported in recent years, until that night.

Margaret Monaghan ran into the clubroom screaming. 'I've just seen the ghost,' she shouted. 'I nearly died. It was horrible.'

She went on to describe a hunched figure in a grey duffel coat with the hood up, as she thought. But after further thought, she realised it was a monk in a hooded cloak. It seemed to be trying to push its way through the wall.

'I thought it was Charlie Dorwood (the church gravedigger), and when I said, "Hiya Charlie", it turned round and faced me. It was horrible. It had no eyes or nose.'

'How did it smell?' giggled Rory Quiggley.

'You think I'm joking don't you, well I'm not, I was terrified. Look I'm still trembling.'

Another sighting was reported the next night, and two others subsequently the following night. I think I saw it but couldn't swear to it.

Anyhow the upshot of it all was an exorcism would be needed to rid the club of this horrid ghoul. Joan and Margaret were convinced we'd disturbed it by making use of the hitherto abandoned rooms, and it didn't like it. The description of our ghost fitted rather neatly with the description of the legendary monk who had lived in the Old Priory and occasionally surfaced to frighten off intruders.

LITTLE IRELAND

Father McCann was informed, and he instructed Father Leonard to dispense his services and force this unwelcome visitor to rest its weary soul once and for all.

On Monday night at 6pm he arrived, having not had very far to travel, some twenty yards or so from the back door of the presbytery. He performed a very serious and animated exorcism using candles and holy water and lashings of 'Get ye gone to your holy rest' phrases.

We never saw the ghost again.

The club met most nights. We had no formal opening times. We were just a small group of friends opening up when we arrived and closing when we decided to go home. Within a few weeks the membership had risen from a handful to over thirty, and was fast becoming out of control. Because of this, and Father McCann complaining about the noise late at night, the committee was forced to set down some club rules and formalise the opening and closing times. It was decided we needed some adult input, but we would have lost the casual, free and easy atmosphere the club had become famous for. The club staggered on for several more months.

When eventually it happened, Father McCann shouted very angrily, 'Have you got a fire on up there, you lot?'

To which we all replied, 'No Father.'

'Then why are flames bouncing three feet high out of the skylight?' he asked.

It was a fair cop, I had to face him and take my punishment like a man.

That particular night had had a downer on it already. At 7pm the regular transmission of 'Pick of the Pops' had been interrupted to announce the assassination of President Kennedy, which had taken place at 3.30 that afternoon, and America and Britain were in a state of mourning. The promise and future of America seemed to be riding on this charismatic young president with his beautiful wife. The girls cried out loud and the boys shook their heads in disbelief. Such was the popularity of this living legend.

Father McCann dragged me over the coals for my treachery, and made me feel so ashamed of my deception. He insisted I serve 7.30 Mass every morning for a month, and he would consider other disciplinary action - which he never actually did. I'm sure he had a soft spot for me.

Well. it was an accident waiting to happen I suppose. We were lucky to get off so lightly, but while it lasted the Priory Club was a great success and my first real leadership role.

3
RORY QUIGGLEY

About that time we were being taught at school about the pigmies and the mau-maus eating each other. At least that's what Rory Quiggley said.

Mind you, he wasn't very reliable. He took Larty's hound dogs out on Saturday mornings, and told me he would give me half of his shilling for walking the dogs if I went with him round the fell road. I did and he's never paid me yet, and when we got home my mother killed me and sent me to bed. She'd had half the backs out looking for me for two hours.

Rory was a bit of a bugger. He was from a very nice family but somehow totally 'off his head'. His grandma, Mrs Foy, was a sweet old lady, quite stern but with a soft side. She used to come down the garden path to Larty's hut (where we used to play without permission) and lambaste us for twenty minutes about how we'd go to Hell for not doing as we were told, and somehow I always got the impression that this telling off was being carried forward from a more serious one Rory had previously had. Then she would suddenly mellow and give us a sweet and promise of money if we were good lads.

When Stephen and myself became altar boys, Rory's mam taught us the Latin response to the Mass. She'd been a schoolteacher; she was kind and sort of Irish-posh. They lived in the big house at the top of Trumpet Terrace.

There was a swing over Hen Beck, just below where Rory lived, and we used to sneak over to it early in the morning before the Brookside lads got to it, because for some reason Rory wasn't very popular with those lads and they chased us if we went near the swing when they were using it.

The swing was a very thick rope which had been given to us by Paul Dunn's dad, Jim. He used to work at the pit and he lost his leg in a pit accident, so he had a pot one. Paul used to keep his marbles in the spare leg and scare the life out of us when he used to throw it down the stairs at us. He had an Afghan hound called Tara. She was so elegant. Her ears were so long and blonde she looked a bit like Jayne Mansfield - only slim.

LITTLE IRELAND

The swing was yards and yards long. It was tied to the branch of a very large sycamore. It was hung up into the centre of the tree, and you could swing from the bank on one side, let go, and most of the time land on the opposite bank. The beck being about fifteen to twenty feet wide at this point, and about six feet deep in the middle. This point in the river was near the bottom of Trumpet Terrace, opposite Mrs Murray's shop over the sandstone wall just beside the telephone box.

The big lads had loads of different jumps they could do. If you held the last knot in the rope and ran in the opposite direction then hurled yourself out into the river, you could do a full circle swing and land back on the bank about twenty feet on the other side of the tree. Or a shorter swing using the knots higher up the rope, swing out, come back and push yourself back off the tree with your feet, and back over the beck again. If you were very daring, using the piece of wood tied at the end of the rope to form a bar, you could hang upside down by your legs and be pushed out over the beck by some of your trusted friends. Not Raymond Gaithwaite! He persuaded me to have a go and when I was in position, pulled me right up the bank and didn't just let me go, but hurled me out over the beck.

I shot out like some mad trapeze artiste at a hundred-miles-an-hour, shot back and landed head first back into the trunk of the tree. Remember, I was upside down at the time. I saw stars for about ten minutes, had a beauty of a bump on my forehead and became the Brookside hero overnight.

Mind you it has to be said that in the main the big lads were mostly very responsible and concerned for the safety of the younger lads in the group. I always had a feeling of well-being in these groups. The natural leaders among the older lads seemed to be so wise and no-one seemed to question any decision they made.

I think Raymond Gaithwaite lost some credibility that day, but his loss was my gain.

Of course, childhood memories are full of never-ending hot summer days and a carefree existence full of joy, the safety of a loving family and perfect health. Mine was *really* like this. How lucky I was.

One of the things that is so very evocative of those days are scents. Every time I smell a hyacinth I'm back in Bluebell Wood. My Bluebell Wood was halfway between Hen Beck Bridge and Blackhow Farm on the Fell Road.

LITTLE IRELAND

The first time I saw the sea of pale blue flowers, one spring morning in 1955, I thought I'd died and gone to heaven. Even at the age of seven I was so moved by the sheer beauty of this sight. I remember bending down and picking up a handful, drawing them to my face and smelling the heavy musky scent. Just divine. I couldn't verbalise my thoughts at the time, but the memory of it still stays with me to this day.

The woodland at this point wasn't very dense, mainly spruce and larch and a few rowans, and to add to the magical quality, a sprinkle of rhododendrons. Even as a child I knew instinctively that they didn't mix with the natural trees and must have been planted - maybe by some rich prince who wanted to make a special garden for his princess. Or maybe Clem Mossop shoved them in when he was bulldozing one of the farm buildings. I don't know, but they certainly made a perfect setting for the bluebells.

4
MY SISTER MARGARET

My very first recollection was, in fact, of the birth of my sister Margaret. I was three years old, my twin brother Stephen was three years and twenty minutes old - because he came first - and Barry was thirteen months older than both of us.

Nanna Heron introduced us to our new sister by saying, 'Look what the stork dropped onto the garden lads. Your Dad found her under a rhubarb leaf.'

I was mesmerised by this beautiful bundle of softness. I remember wondering where Mam was, and what all the coming-and-going with Aunty May and Aunty Winnie was all about. I spent days wandering round the garden looking under rhubarb leaves. Then nothing registered for another two-and-a-half years. At least I remember nothing until that fateful day.

My sister Margaret was a toddler and quite a madam. She had long brown ringlets and a beautiful complexion. I was so proud of her. Mam let us take her for walks up and down the backs at Prospect Row where we lived.

I remember I had to persuade Mam to let me take Margaret for a walk to the churchyard and back; a walk of about 300 yards. Mam wasn't going to let me at first, but after a lot of persuasion eventually relented. I loved showing her off.

'Just to the churchyard and back mind you, no further,' Mam said. And I reassured her, that's as far as I would go.

Margaret wasn't a bit tired when we arrived at the church gates some five minutes later. So I lifted her onto the wall and held her hand until we reached the bridge over the Lonnie Beck. It was a narrow, flat, concrete bridge with stout cast-iron railings running the length of both sides. I loved tumbling over the middle rail. Mam used to go mad when she saw me do this. She said I'd fall in the beck one of these days, but I knew I wouldn't fall in. I was five-and-a-half, and I could do handstands!

My cousin Shaun Devoy's grandfather had the garden overlooking the Lonnie Bridge. Shaun called him 'Cleator Daddy', so that's what we all called him.

LITTLE IRELAND

The garden had a huge privet hedge round it except for the side overlooking the beck and the cricket field beyond. On warm Sunday afternoons Cleator Daddy and Mrs Devoy could be seen from the cricket pavilion sitting on their brightly coloured striped, canvas deck chairs and with their straw hats on, enjoying the sunshine and listening to the gentle purr of enthusiasm drifting over from the gentlemanly spectators watching Cleator playing Cockermouth, Wigton or Penrith.

These days were very dream-like to me. I had no interest in the game; it all seemed so slow and dreary. My mind would wander to the spectators and the distant views. I discovered the third wood on the side of Dent was almost in the shape of a squirrel, and that Black Wood was exactly like a large black bell.

Elsie Roony and Peggy Graham and their loyal band of helpers made the tea and sandwiches for the players and everybody was very hospitable to the Away Team and their coach-load of supporters. Life on cricket field Sundays seemed to be in a time warp to me. I needed much more excitement to stimulate my growing mind.

Cleator Daddy was a man of very few words. I suspect he didn't really like children. We were only allowed into the garden when Shaun was with us. I think we were all a bit frightened of him, but it was worth the fear for me to see inside this fascinating and secret garden.

The garden was south facing and an absolute sun trap because of its impenetrable privet hedge giving it shelter to an otherwise very open site. I use the word 'impenetrable' because we used to try to poke a hole in it to see what was on the other side, but with very little success. It wasn't like the allotment gardens opposite our house, which were cluttered with old tin sheeting sheds and tumble-down hen huts.

It was the first time I'd seen a formal garden laid out with symmetrical herbaceous borders, furnished with rows of wallflowers, Sweet Williams and dahlias, surrounded by perfect box hedges. It had a well-cut lawn where the couple used to sit in their deck chairs, and had a greenhouse with a coke boiler. The peppery smell of tomato plants and sulphur from the stove clung to your nostrils when you entered the greenhouse through a creosoted wooden tunnel, decorated with garden utensils hanging up in neat rows on the

LITTLE IRELAND

boarded walls, along with a faded yellow and green parasol.

I don't know why I was so afraid of Cleator Daddy because I don't remember ever hearing him say a word; either to his wife or to anybody else, including Shaun for that matter. Maybe it was the fear of the unknown.

The shutter was off Cleator Daddy's garden gate that morning as we passed by, so I assumed he must be in, digging his tatties out or clipping his hedges in his quiet way.

When we arrived at the bridge, to my surprise and absolute delight, the beck was in flood. My eyes were out like organ stops. It was apparent the lads had been fishing for eels because the bank had that earthy sweet smell of trampled wet grass and damp soil.

I did my ritual tumble over the middle rail and found myself excited at the thought of coming down later with Joe Farren, my next door neighbour. He was eight and helped me make my line for catching eels. Joe was alright, he knew about everything. He could build bogies, sledges, kites and mice hutches. He bred white mice with pink eyes, and could tell a buck from a doe at thirty yards.

The only problem was, Joe used to kill the eels and I hated that, but the excitement of being with him outweighed the horror of this spectacle. Albert Palmer said, 'You should just let them back into the water, because next time the beck is in flood you'd be able to catch them again, only they'd be bigger.'

I went along with his philosophy.

It must have been midday by now, and we should have been back home for our dinner, but with all the excitement of the beck being flooded and everything else, I'd forgotten the time and about our Margaret until, that is, I heard a loud 'plop'. Not a splash, you understand.

The water at this time was nearly level with the surface of the bridge so anything being thrown into it or falling into it from the bridge wouldn't make a loud 'splash' - just a 'plop'!

This loud plop brought me out of my daydream and I thought to myself, 'Where's Margaret?'

I know I said I heard the plop first, but I was only five-and-a-half, and the events that were to follow have somewhat clouded my memory, because I have a vague recollection of seeing her do a topple over the middle rail, as she must have seen me doing earlier, or I just saw her feet disappear over the edge of the bridge. I can't be sure, but the sound and the sight seemed to come together.

My first reaction was one of numbness. Everything was suddenly happening in slow motion.

Why had I not seen the obvious danger I had put her in, leaving her on her own and turning my back on her? She couldn't be in the water! I scanned the bridge and the Lonnie on either side of it, knowing she must be nearby. I could hear my heart beating, filling my head with a sickening thud. A log was coming down stream at a rate of knots towards the bridge, with a branch sticking up in midair. It hit the bottom of the bridge and disappeared under it.

I turned round to see it re-appear on the other side and saw Margaret floating face down several yards down stream. Her arms were spread out as if she were trying to stop herself from sinking, but they didn't seem to be moving.

My second reaction was to run into Cleator Daddy's garden and shout for help.

My precise memories of the following events are a bit of a blur because I sort of remember seeing Mr Lancaster in the distance with his dog, and screaming at him to hurry up. Yet at the same time I was back at Prospect Row seeing Dad rushing past me, heading toward the beck on a child's bike. I couldn't face the horror of seeing Margaret drifting even further away down stream, and must have blocked out those few minutes from my memory.

People were running past me. I knew it was my fault and I knew she was dead. I was trying to turn the clock back, thinking if only I hadn't let go of her hand. If only I'd gone back home after the churchyard when I was supposed to and not got carried away.

Suddenly I was out of the initial shock which block out your emotions and into the next stage of shock. The reality of facing up to what had happened, and I was beside myself with grief, but unable to cry. My chest was bursting and yet my tears wouldn't come. The result of this was me running to Joe Farren's garden and hiding in his hut.

I sat on the floor looking at the floorboards and listening to the pet mice scratching in their nest boxes for what seemed like hours, but in fact was probably only minutes.

Joe used to tell me never to let the buck in with the doe when she

LITTLE IRELAND

had young, because the buck would eat them. I remember thinking this as I opened the cage door and put the buck into the nest box with the doe and five young. Nothing mattered any more. This place was the perfect place to hide; it stank of mouse droppings and pee and was perfectly appropriate to my mood of absolute despair - cold, dank and dark.

I could see the buck poking the young with its nose and moving them out of the nest onto the bare sawdust peppered floor of the cage. It seemed to want the nest for itself. Then suddenly the doe appeared and the buck started to mate with her. The young ones were squeaking and scratching their weak legs against the bare floorboards, trying to get back to the nest, but they could hardly move from where they were. The buck had had its fill and started to nip at the heads of the nearest young, when I realised suddenly that Joe was right. I picked it up and put it back into its own cage and slowly replaced the young into their nest. The doe hurriedly pushed the soft shredded newspaper back over them and devotedly started her motherly duties once again.

I thought how cheap life is to a mouse. How could he want to kill his own young? Perhaps he didn't realise they were his, but why did he want to kill them any way? I didn't want our Margaret to be dead, but she was and it was *entirely* my fault.

Then I heard a voice softly saying, 'Sean are you in there?'

I recognised the voice, it was Mrs Maudsley. She had the fish and chip shop on the corner of Main Street and Church Went. Her husband had the allotment next to Joe's where he kept his hounds. Mr Maudsley used to run them at the hound trail. He hadn't won a trail for years, Dad said, and when the hounds were too old to run he used to keep them as pets in his big hut on the allotment. Uncle Eddie said that he must be off his head; they should be put down as soon as they stop running.

Mr Maudsley used to let me take Meg, the old bitch, for a walk on a lead which seemed to be ten feet long and six inches wide, made of leather, with a strong steel clasp.

Mrs Maudlsey opened the hut door. She had seen me running into the hut when she was feeding the dogs and had heard our Barry shouting for me.

'Come on Sean, you needn't hide in there, no-one's blaming you. Your mother is looking all over for you. I'll take you home,' she said.

I remember the feeling of relief. She was a kind, gentle woman and my hand in hers felt safe, and I felt slightly reassured.

The walk back to our house seemed like an eternity. Mrs Maudsley kept tight hold of my hand, and I wasn't sure whether this was to stop me from running away or to make me feel secure. My thoughts were focused on her strong grip and the bright sunlight. For a few minutes I couldn't really see anything at all.

The short walk from Joe's garden along the mud path led to the backs of Church Went with its rough sandstone backyard walls. Some of the yard gates were falling off from lack of repair and all of them except Mr McAvoy's needed a good painting. Mr McAvoy bred Yorkshire terriers. He also showed them and could often be seen going up Main Street on his bike with three or four of them in the front basket, all sitting perfectly still like soft toys.

His gate was open and a sight I'd only seen once before, and could hardly believe it then, had presented itself again. The Yorkies had very long thick hair, trailing on the ground; they were always immaculately groomed with a red ribbon on their topknots.

That day was obviously washday because Mr McAvoy had three of the dogs hanging on the line to dry. They just swung peacefully in the breeze, twisting their heads round now and again to see who was passing by. The Mass of long hair on their backs was wrapped over the washing line and held in place with a series of wooden clothes pegs. The poor wee things didn't seem to be distressed in any way, but it did seem a cruel way to keep them clean while their hair dried.

This seemed to highlight my feeling of anxiety and I carried on walking in a state of panic until we turned the corner into Prospect Row backs and saw what looked like a sea of people standing around our back gate.

The yard was full of neighbours, people were trying to see into the yard from the backs. Everybody suddenly went quiet as soon as they saw me. Mrs Fleming from next door took my other hand and said, 'Come on lad your Mam's in the house waiting for you.'

Mrs Maudsley released my hand and I saw Mam running towards me. She picked me up and we both started to cry. She said those six words I'll never forget, 'Margaret is going to be alright.'

I stopped breathing for a few seconds to concentrate on her words. It hadn't occurred to me that she could be alive. I saw her floating downstream face down and motionless. It must have been a miracle.

Well, a miracle it may well have been, because if Mr Lancaster from Church Went hadn't heard me shout and come running just in time to see Margaret washed up on the rapids and waded in to get her; then she would have been dead. He struggled against the force of the water with Margaret in his arms. Fortunately by this time Dad had arrived on the scene and managed to haul Mr Lancaster out. He was an elderly man and the whole experience exhausted him.

The next half-hour had been critical because Margaret was unconscious. Dad ran home with her in his arms and Papa Heron and Dad revived her by placing her in a bath of hot water and a bath of cold water alternately for some time until she was breathing normally again.

Normality seemed to be restored to our household almost immediately. I remember Mam very calmly saying to Dad, 'Take Mr Lancaster a wee glass of whisky Jay and thank him for his help. The poor old man could have been drowned himself.'

5
THE CHURCH

Needless to say church played a large part in our lives, being practising Catholics.

It has been pointed out to me in recent years that Catholics in other places can feel marginalised, because they are in the minority. Not at Cleator forty years ago, I would say about fifty/fifty or perhaps even seventy-five/twenty-five to the Catholics. And our very large Catholic Church, St Mary's at Cleator was my home-from-home. I don't have an early recollection of it because I would have been taken there from a very early age and it became the epicentre of my world and stood for all the things that I believed in. 'Give me the boy at seven and I will give you the man', said The Jesuits. How true.

The formative years filled my mind and soul with Catholic belief. After some barren years spiritually speaking, I returned to the practice of my faith, and continue my weekly visits to Mass at St Mary's to this day.

Protestants were viewed with suspicion by my parents and grandparents, although we being fourth generation Irish immigrants my feelings were somewhat diluted and I had one or two Protestant friends. We were not allowed to go into a Protestant church, to any of the services, I think under the threat of ex-communication. So when I had an opportunity to see inside a Protestant church legitimately, I jumped at the chance.

St Leonard's Church of England church at Cleator was only thirty to forty yards from my home in Prospect Row. Down the back street on to Church Went, turn left at the Jubilee Rooms and you were there. The churchyard was surrounded by a rather splendid sandstone wall which had once had cast-iron railings on top of it, but these were removed during the war and sent to be melted down to make tanks for the war effort. So many beautiful railings had been lost forever for this reason. Every town and village in England lost some of the finest cast-ironworks depicting their heritage to the bloody war effort. I suppose it's easy to romanticise now, but in 1940 when bombs were being dropped on every major city in England, and Hitler was making inroads through Europe, people gladly sacrificed these pieces of metal. But I can't help regretting their loss.

The church had a beautiful lych-gate, and I had literally never stepped beyond this gate. We were doing a project at school about historical buildings, including churches. The project included some field studies and visits to the particular buildings you had decided to use as your study. I went for St Leonard's. I had to contact the caretaker Mrs Malaghan, in order to arrange a mutually convenient time to look both outside and inside the church. Mrs Malaghan - Joan - was not the least bit formidable. In fact, she was very approachable, and quite touched at the thought of me, a Catholic, wanting to know anything about St Leonard's. The date and time was set, 2.30pm, Wednesday next. Then I needn't go back to school afterwards.

There were three students who decided on St Leonard's as their subject. Arthur McGlaughlin, Pat Flemming and myself. We were greeted by Mrs Malaghan and after opening the main doors to let us into the church she said, 'I'll be knocking about doing my cleaning Sean, if there's anything you want to know just ask.'

Well prior to the visit, which was mainly to give us a feel for the building, and to do some sketches of the stained glass and the various religious *objets d'arts,* and indeed the building from outside, we had already completed the study of the actual history of the building from its inception in the year 1185 to the present building, completed in 1903. And we knew all about its fate at the hands of Henry VIII during the Dissolution of the Monasteries and the Reformation. Some of the gravestones also were of particular interest because they dated back to 1735, and the sense of history surrounding the place was tangible.

I asked some pertinent questions of our very agreeable hostess, and she obligingly gave me the answers to the best of her knowledge. Then she asked me what I knew of St Leonard's, to which I answered, 'Well, a church was built on this site in 1185, some of the chancel and altar still remain to this day, and it has been used as a church ever since that date, being rebuilt probably several times. Finally the present building was built in the year 1903. So, before 1650, it would have been a Catholic church.'

Well, talk about the shit hitting the fan: 'This chuch has nivver been a Catholic chuch,' shrieked Mrs Malaghan. 'It's always been a Protestant chuch, now go on git yersels away 'ome now, I've got to git on. I've nivver 'eard owt like it in me life. A Catholic chuch, nivver.'

Now this thing about Catholics and Protestants, although as I said earlier, was being diluted by each successive generation, still existed when I was a lad. For instance, the Flosh Cottages at Cleator, about twelve houses in all, some of which were built in the seventeenth century, later ones added in the eighteenth and nineteenth centuries, to form a small row of cottages. A very pleasant little row of English cottages with a wide pavement in front of them. They were occupied by the Protestant fraternity. There were the Jardines and the Greggs, and so on and so on. All staunch Church of England.

Outside the Jardines, number 10, was a metal ring fixed into the wall at about shoulder height, which was used to tether a horse in the olden days. In fact, Andrew Watson used to tether his milk float to it every morning in life, much to our annoyance, because we had a tradition, the schoolchildren that is, if you were a Catholic, to put the ring into the upright position, indicating Heaven, and if you were a Protestant, the down position, indicating Hell, or so the Catholics believed. So when Andrew Watson confused matters by tethering the leather bridle of his milk float to it, no one knew whether a Catholic or a Protestant was the last one to pass by the Flosh Cottages. What a drag!

St Mary's School, Cleator, which I attended, was a disused church, formerly St Bega's, and when the new church in the Gothic style was built in 1872 to replace it, it became St Mary's School. It wasn't really wholly suitable as a school for many reasons, one of which was that there was no main hall and consequently nowhere to hold a full assembly. So, very little contact was made between classes, and the teachers in the class above you were an unknown entity, except for horrendous folklore, which was passed down to us from the older lads, such as 'Miss Cairns gives you a kidney punch if you misbehave.'

I rather think she was probably capable of this, but never actually saw her do it, although I occasionally saw Brian Fletcher mysteriously disappear under his desk after a short and swift visit from behind from Miss Cairns. She never left a mark.

We had Mrs Nolan our infant teacher, a middle-aged lady very kind and motherly. I was fond of her, probably one of the best and nicest teachers I ever had, although on my very first day at school I remember all the children in my class, and their mothers sort of linked up to go into the classroom together. No nursery or pre-school groups in those days, you went in cold. Most of the kids were holding frantically to their mother's hand knowing that eventually they would have to let go and be marched into class. All seemed to be going well until Julie Farren decided she'd had enough. She started to cry.

Her Mam reassured her and said, 'You'll be alright Julie, Mrs Nolan will look after you pet, and Sean and Stephen are here. And you'll be able to see our Margaret at playtime.'

To no avail, the cry progressed into a sob and then into a wail, and eventually into a scream. Mrs Nolan approached and said, 'Now then Julie, this will never do, you have to come to school, now be a good girl and come along with me'.

To which Julie replied, 'Get away from me, I want my Mam.'

Mrs Nolan was very patient but had to show her some firmness, so she took hold of both of her hands and knelt down in front of her in order to make Julie feel less threatened. This didn't work because Julie let fly with her right foot and caught Mrs Nolan a direct hit on her left knee. Mrs Nolan responded to this by slapping her quite hard on the legs. This only exacerbated the situation, because Julie laid into her with both feet and both fists. Mrs Nolan was visibly shaken and Julie was ballistic.

Her Mam intervened at this point and took her out of the room. I felt sick, Stephen was crying, along with probably every other child in the room, and I remember looking up at my Mam, who had a tear in her eye, and thinking, please, please don't leave me here.

That was the first day.

The next day wasn't so bad and eventually we had to accept that it is a way of life for the next ten years.

I can't in truth say my school days were happy days. Some of them were extremely unhappy at times. I felt desperate, and a total victim. You went from Mrs Nolan's 'Infants', to Miss Cairns `Junior', and then Mr McCrickard's 'Top junior'.

If I'm to be honest I have to say I was absolutely terrified of Mr McCrickard. The stories filtering down from the big lads were horrendous. Phrases like, 'Which pain do you want to go through?' and `Go on, lad, pick your pain.'

I didn't think I could cope with this man, clothed in Harris tweed three-piece suits, very smart. He had a moss-green one, a terracotta-red one and a slate-grey one. I never actually heard him use his catchphrase on anyone, but I was aware of the strictness shown to all

- boys and girls alike.

The desks were old-fashioned, a bench and a lid covering a box suitable for books etc., all held together with a cast-iron, ornately decorated frame. The seat was hinged and could be lifted up in order to stand to attention. Many a time, Brian Fletcher was hurled up by the front of his jumper, his clogs clattering through the wooden seat, as he was held shoulder high by the throat, and then dropped back down by 'Crado', Mr McCrickard's nickname. Nor did Susan McAvoy escape the wrath of this man; she received the treatment on several occasions.

Of course, the good and the bad memories remain longest with us, and if a particular event made an impression or left a scar, we never forgot it. It's sometimes hard to reconcile these violent acts on the one hand with the very genuine true Christian values taught to us by the same people. But the thread that runs through my school life with my various teachers, good and bad, binds together human failings, forgiveness and reconciliation.

They taught us the teachings of Christ and the academic lessons required to the best of their ability. I don't think at that time people were aware of the victims they were leaving in their wake. Today of course, things have turned full circle.

6
OLD CRADO DOES HIS WORST

As I said before, the practice of the Catholic religion played a huge part in my childhood. We had to be very knowledgeable in church doctrine from an early age. We needed to know what a 'sacrament' was, what was meant by a 'mortal' sin and avoid the occasion of sin - so Protestants could be loosely described as the occasion of sin. They swore and gave cheek to old people, they stole things and bullied Catholics. They called us 'Catholic cats' and we responded by calling them 'Prody dogs', so they were best avoided.

We had lots of prayers to learn off by heart: 'Our Father', 'Hail Mary', 'Apostles Creed', 'Nicene Creed', 'The Magnificat', an 'Act of Contrition', 'I Believe', 'Glory Be', 'Grace' before and after meals, and dozens more. We could rattle them off like a parrot, without even thinking.

We had to learn them because we never knew when Father McCann, or Father Clayton, might call into school and put you on the spot: 'Now Sean, I'm sure a good Catholic boy like you from a good Catholic family can say an Act of Contrition. So would you like to stand up and let the whole class hear you in a good loud voice?'

This was Father Clayton. It happened to me on several occasions and thanks be to God, I was word perfect. If I'd flunked it Mr McCrickard would have leathered me for showing him up, and he wouldn't tolerate that.

The worst experience in my entire school life occurred one cold February morning. We had a spelling test every Friday morning. We'd be given a dozen or so new words to learn and we had a week to learn them. Friday was my nightmare day. I had a mental block about certain words, bordering on word blindness, but Old Crado had decided I was just too lazy to learn the words. The truth was my problem hadn't been detected by Miss Cairns or Mr McCrickard, so I wasn't offered any special tuition. There was a missing link and try as I may, I couldn't make the connection. It hampered me no end when I was writing compositions. My story would be very clear to me in my head and my grammar and punctuation was good, but the spelling was terrible. I used to skirt round words, putting words I could spell in place of the ones I really wanted to use.

LITTLE IRELAND

I felt tortured in my young mind, because I was embarrassed about it. I hated being made a show of in front of the rest of the class.

This particular day, Crado excelled himself in the humiliation stakes. My mental block was Saturday, I'd written 'SATERDAY'. He looked down at my paper and leaned right down with his face up to mine. I could smell his breath and see the blue edge of his hard lips and the membrane of spit that was always in the corner of his mouth when he spoke, like a translucent skin. He had a very distinctive habitual cough, it was more a throat clearing exercise. He was renowned for it. When he got close to being annoyed he'd give this one single rattle, and you were suddenly on your guard. The room would instantly go silent, as the annoyance grew the frequency of the rattle increased in length and depth and God help whoever it was directed at!

He got hold of me by the ear and pulled me to my feet. I thought my ear was coming off. He then let go and did his rattle several times then screamed at me, 'How have you spelt 'Saturday', boy?'

I mustered up every bit of self-composure against a heartbeat that had almost deafened me to make my answer. I said, 'S..A..T..E..R..D..A..Y, sir.'

He continued his rattle and his face became so distorted with rage I thought, even hoped, he was having a heart attack. I was ashamed, I couldn't see the word in my mind, I could have tried for a full day and still never put a 'u' in Saturday. Maybe an 'a', or even an 'i', but never a 'u'.

He calmed himself slightly and asked between rattles, 'Who's the youngest in the class?'

Susan McAvoy said, 'I am, sir.'

He told Susan to spell 'Saturday', and she answered, 'S..A..T..U..R..D..A..Y, sir.'

He thanked Susan and told her to sit down again, amid further rattles. He told the rest of the class to stay silent for five minutes until he got back, then literally dragged me with him through the door to Miss Cairns' class. It was the one below mine; she taught Standard 1 and 2. I was in Standard 4.

Old Crado excused himself to Miss Cairns for interrupting her class and proceeded to tell the children that he had a boy with him who was in Standard 4 but who couldn't spell Saturday. He asked for the youngest pupil in Standard 1 and 2 to come to the front and spell Saturday. They both spelt the letters out together - S..A..T..U..R..D..A..Y.

I could feel myself sliding deeper into a sense of hopelessness and deep despair. I thought I was going to pass out. I was physically sick into my mouth and was gently crying to myself. He had humiliated me beyond anything I could have imagined. I was truly stunned. He muttered between rattles, 'Now, maybe you'll remember how to spell it in future, boy.'

That night, I was sick several times in my bed for no apparent reason, and the following morning Mam let me stay off school for the day to see how my stomach upset went on.

I was relieved beyond belief, and had another couple of days off for good measure, because I'd put my fingers down my throat and brought several meals back up. If I'd stayed in his class for much longer I would have made a habit of the regurgitating trick and God knows where that would have led to. I had been systematically dehumanised and this was to have a profound effect on the rest of my school life.

My mother used to put a 'Miraculous Medal' onto our vests, and I remember fingering the medal after my punishment and saying a prayer to Our Lady to help me survive the rest of the day and to help me to forgive him, which eventually I did.

7
MISS CAIRNS

Here we go again you're thinking, another character assassination. Not at all.

Miss Cairns was really quite kind, and although rather stern looking, had a soft side to her nature. She had a penchant for purple, from shades of mauve and lilac to dark red and regal purple. Wearing large shift-type dresses with fancy pleated bodices buttoned up to the neck, often with a lace collar, always long and flowing. She looked as if she was in 'widow's weeds'.

I think the unspoken threat of a sudden kidney punch from behind, and her Edwardian governess dress sense, reinforced my opinion that Miss Cairns should be treated with respect. And indeed she was. So pity help anyone who didn't get this message straight away.

Our old school didn't have many creature comforts, we had gaslights on a long bar suspended from the high ceiling, with a cluster of half-a-dozen mantles at both ends. It used to give off a yellow glow and quite a lot of heat. But the main heating system was a pot-bellied stove in the centre of the classroom. By half-past two in the afternoon, after seven or eight hours of constant use, it would be literally glowing bright red.

Miss Cairns used to be a fantastic storyteller, and in the late afternoon on Friday, if we had been good, she would read us a story from the *'Arabian Nights'* or *'Big Claws and Little Claws'*. She would become very animated and quite carried away. I saw her in a different light. She was a large lady with generous bosoms, and when you're seven there's something rather comforting about large bosoms combined with the late afternoon sun drifting into the classroom and the distinctive smell gas lights which cast shadows on the magnolia-coloured walls. Coupled with the unreal, mythical *'Arabian Nights'* stories, the atmosphere all-too-often lent itself to sleep, only to be awakened by the sudden rush of air following the board rubber, which always seemed to miss its intended target and hit the poor unsuspecting Wilfy Rogers, who was sitting next to me. This would be followed by Miss Cairns rushing for the first aid box amid a tirade of verbal abuse aimed at me, 'Just wait until I sort out Wilfy'. Oh, no not the kidney punch!

We had very little in the way of physical exercise, no hall for PE, but once or twice a term if the weather allowed us, we would be marched out in rows onto the playground and given a raffia mat and two bean bags. These bean bags were filled with hard beans I suppose, and I was never quite sure of their purpose, except they added a certain tactile quality to the sessions.

Miss Cairns then instructed us to place the mats in front of us all in regimented lines and lie down on them. This we would do, amid whispers of, 'I can see Peggy Eldon's knickers,' from Paul Dunn, and Peggy saying, 'Miss, Paul Dunn is looking up my skirt,' Hughie Doran farting straight into Ian Payne's face and getting a fist in his back, and Linda Williamson shouting, 'My bean bag's split, Miss.'

No wonder we only did PE twice a term.

Then we'd stand up and Miss Cairns would stand in front of us and hold the bean bags straight in front of her, and do a knee bend continuing to hold her arms in the same position.

It was hysterical, we could hardly contain ourselves. This huge woman, who had replaced her formal Cuban-heeled leather boots for a pair of brilliant white sandshoes, attempting to lower her ample frame to the floor via a knees bend, looked so incongruous that we couldn't take her seriously. I mean, it can't be right. We needed a lithe, youthful PE instructor, not old Abby Cairns, good as she is reading the 'Arabian Nights' and teaching us hymns, such as 'Hail Glorious St Patrick' and 'Sweet Heart of Jesus', from a sitting position her PE instructions lacked credibility and dignity. Our Miss Cairns was better in the classroom and, God love her, she knew it. But the mixture of carnival atmosphere and SS-style aerobics was a wonderful twice-termly event.

The Council School was next to our school separated only by a five-foot sandstone wall. This wall served many purposes. You could inadvertently drop a boulder off it on to some poor unsuspecting Protestant - that wasn't even a mortal sin. Or just spit over it and wait for a reaction. But best of all were the snowball fights. Every playtime for the duration of the snow, the 'killing fields' of Cleator opened.

One particular snowy November, the snow had lain for four days

LITTLE IRELAND

and was becoming rather slushy and tired, so to liven up the good-humoured rivalry, Brian Fletcher announced he'd started putting a lump of coke in his snowball to give it a bit more kick. As soon as the Protestants discovered this, their dirty tricks department waded in with both feet and hands - no holds barred. There were marbles, lead sinkers and half bricks in some of them, and Miss Cairns heard the mayhem when she came to blow the whistle for the end of playtime, only to be met by a brilliant snowball carrying a piece of coal, which caught her full in the face and stopped her dead in her tracks. Suddenly, she was like a whirling dervish and a banshee rolled into one. She hurled herself at the enemy, who continued to pelt her with dozens of snowballs, but she was undeterred.

'I'm coming to see Mr McKenzie about this. I'll put a stop to it, and what's your name boy? You'll be punished for this good day.'

After an extended and exciting playtime, Miss Cairns ushered us all back into school, looking quite cross-eyed with her normally very well-coiffured white bun with its fine hairnet keeping every strand in place, looking rather damp and dishevelled.

The lecture we received after returning to our desks was memorable, and this particular incident - the coal in the snowball incident - was worked by Miss Cairns to its best advantage, to illustrate the difference between good and evil, or Catholic and Protestant.

Of course, it was only to be expected, she went on, that the Protestants would resort to putting missiles inside their snowballs, because they didn't know any better. Now you good Catholic boys wouldn't do such a thing, because you do know better. But we should not retaliate in any way. Just feel sorry for them, they were not advantaged the way we were. It's not their fault.

No wonder we thought we were God's chosen people and everyone else was an underclass of heathens.

Miss Cairns, I'm sure, saw her main purpose in life to prepare us for Holy Communion at the age of seven. This she did with a passion. We were well versed in the catechism by now, and the next step was first Confession, on the first Saturday in June, and first Communion on the Sunday at nine o'clock Mass.

Now the preparation for these enormously important sacraments

LITTLE IRELAND

were monumental, equivalent to a mini-degree. In fact, if her teaching methods were adopted today and geared to more academic rather than spiritual subjects, we could be the most brilliantly educated race in the entire world. But, alas, the National Curriculum and Key Stage One, etc., leave a lot to be desired in comparison with her dedicated methods.

Confession was a terrifying prospect at seven, and because we had to know the difference between a 'venal' sin and a 'mortal' sin, and the severity of the punishment to go with them, we were given a list of sins to confess, those a seven-year-old was likely to commit, like telling lies, swearing, disobedience etc.. We also needed to be aware of mortal sins, such as murder, robbery, and missing Mass on Sunday.

I did my first Confession and felt cleansed and received my first Communion the following morning and felt truly full of the Holy Spirit. This high state of spirituality stayed with me into my early teens when conflicting natural urges came into play. But that's another story.

Not everyone had the advantage of a brilliant spiritual teacher like Miss Cairns. One Saturday morning, my younger cousins Jimmy Devoy and Stephen Graham, who didn't attend St Mary's School, were attending Confession.

When Jimmy's turn came, I could hear Father O'Connell, who had a wonderful sense of humour and loved children, chuckling away inside the Confessional Box. Then, stony silence, and Jimmy coming out of the Confessional with a grin on his face like a Cheshire cat. He nudged Stephen, who was about to go in, and said, 'Make up as many sins as you can, because the more sins you've done the more sweets he'll give you.'

I think some fell on stony ground; of course you can't win them all. Miss Cairns would turn in her grave if she knew that story.

Miss Cairns had been off school for three weeks. She'd stapled her finger to the desk and it had taken bad ways. Our temporary teacher was Mrs Monaghan - Nancy.

If I remember correctly, we were Miss Cairn's last class before her retirement. She came to leave without ceremony, but I'm sure there must have been some sort of presentation, which the children would have been in on, but strangely I have no recollection of it.

I saw her many years later trailing round Cleator Moor looking very unkempt and obviously confused. I stopped to talk to her and she couldn't remember me or Stephen or Barry or Margaret. I remember thinking my childhood had never really happened. I was so saddened at the obvious demise of this great character who had diminished both in stature and mental ability almost resembling a bag lady. How cruel life's rich tapestry can be.

8
NANCY WITH THE LAUGHING EYES

Can you be in love at nine years old?

Mrs Monaghan would be about twenty-one years old, fresh out of college and I mean 'fresh'. She was the most beautiful woman I had ever seen. She must have been witty and sophisticated as well as being eager to get to know us all, although I doubt if I recognised these qualities at the time. All I know was that she was lovely. She could relate to me and me to her in a way no other teacher had been able to. She was lively and interesting and intense and colourful, and everything a junior schoolteacher should be and she was young. Sadly, my other teachers had been old, and she was a breath of fresh air.

Miss Cairns had taught us songs like, the *'Harp That Once Through Tara's Halls',* and *'The Last Rose of Summer',* terrible unaccompanied dirges, but Mrs Monaghan could play the piano and we sang fun things like *'My Hat, It Had Five Corners'* and *'Hot Diggety Boom Diggety'.* Her lessons were a gift from God and restored my shattered faith in human nature.

I suspect she realised this and purposely gave us a real good time. Thank you, Mrs Monaghan.

We had outside toilets at St Mary's. They were grim. Three cubicles with very small toilets and a urinal. This urinal was composed of a metal bar the same as the one used for the gas lights, running the length of a short wall about six feet long, with a series of holes drilled at about six inches apart to allow the water to trickle down the cement-rendered wall into a trough at the bottom and to drain away into the sink. The water was only turned on intermittently and on hot summer days passing the bog door was like a visit to the abattoir. I'll leave the details to your imagination.

Being outside in an open yard meant, of course that there was no roof and the playtime entertainment was often seeing who could pee over the wall.

Now a good head of steam was required. A dribble was no good if you were to traverse the sandstone coping-stone at the top of the wall and onto the yard. Being tall helped, no good for me I'm afraid. I could manage it, but I had to control my willie in such a way that it

LITTLE IRELAND

resembled a pea shooter, holding the end tight so as not to let any pee out while I concentrated on bearing down, then let go and 'Hey presto', the Trevi Fountains of St Mary's.

These were pre-pubescent days and everyone entered into the spirit of fun. Fun that is, except for the time when Mr McCrickard, having been summoned by a call of nature, just happened to be passing by the bog wall as Rory Quiggley, who had mustered a head of steam that would have sunk the 'Queen Mary', let fly, just at the very spot where old Crado stood. He got the full force of it in his trilby hat, thankfully, but still wasn't best pleased. He hurled himself into the bog and screamed blue murder at Rory, Joe Youdale, Ian Payne and myself. Surprisingly, no punishment was given, I expected at least 'six of the best' and 'Choose your window boys'. But maybe Crado was amused at these boys' trick, we'll never know.

Now, every time a smell of Jeyes Fluid passes me I think of poor Rory getting caught with his pants down so to speak.

9
THE MISSIONERS

The Missioners used to arrive in Cleator Moor at the beginning of Lent.

They always seemed to be Irish and full of sackcloth and ashes. Not a very happy bunch of fellows at all. But they did a brilliant job of filling us with Catholic guilt: for a full week you got it in the neck.

They had a flair for thumping the crucifix, which hung precariously at the side of the pulpit, and screaming at the top of their voices about 'eternal damnation' and the need to be 'purged' of our sins.

They held nightly sessions with large numbers of the faithful attending each session. I reckoned if you made it through that week of Hell, you would be well and truly purged of your sins.

Then, at the end of the Mission, you went to confession to one of the missioners, and for your penance it wasn't the three Our Fathers and one Hail Mary, Father McCann used to dole out. You could see little old ladies coming out of the confessional sobbing, throwing themselves against the altar rails and remaining there prostrate for thirty-six hours. I dread to think what they could have done to deserve such penance, but at least they had a full year to go back to their sins and debauchery before they had to face the `hit squad' again.

Father McCann had two special things he did during Lent, that I know of. He never slept in his bed for the duration, he slept in a chair in his room or in the vestry and he didn't wear any shoelaces in his shoes. So every time he genuflected during Mass or whenever he passed the church altar, the shoe remained flat to the ground and his bare heel scraped out of it, often revealing a big tattie in his black sock. You could hear him clonking along long before you saw him. It was his outward sign of penance and reminded everybody of their duty to do penance during Lent. He was a saint with a sense of humour.

Stephen and I used to serve Mass from an early age, and knew Father McCann well. He loved a good laugh, but some of his jokes went right over me. I used to laugh at them for fear of offending him, but he was a pleasure to be with, very approachable and kind to children. He knew every child by name, he'd probably christened

LITTLE IRELAND

most of them, and their names were indelibly printed on his brain.

We were once in the vestry on a Monday evening getting ready to deliver the weekly Father McCann's sweep tickets. He used to take a group of lads every Monday night with him in his car and drop us off at strategic points around Cleator Moor armed with bundles of tickets which we would deliver to various ticket distributors around the town. He'd wait for us and take us back to the church from where we made our own way home.

On this occasion Ma Murphy was practising on the church organ and Father McCann in his dry sort of way said, 'Ah, there's Mary playing the organ with her elbows again', and a little chuckle followed. I think that was one of his jokes, so we all laughed and smiled at each other thinking that must be a really funny joke.

Our Stephen had gone to confession one Saturday morning and such were his sins he decided he didn't want Father McCann to recognise his voice so he decided to disguise it by putting a hankie over his mouth to muffle his voice. He made his confession and was given absolution thinking he'd got away with it. He rose to leave when Father McCann said, 'Oh, by the way Stephen, we're short of a server for half-past seven Mass on Monday morning, you won't mind standing in will you?'

Stephen said, 'Father, no, of course I'll tell my Mam to get me up', and left feeling a bit of a dickhead.

I bet Father McCann had a good old chuckle at Stephen's expense when he had the confessional to himself. You see you got away with nowt.

You know the joke about the three old ladies and the acrobat saying their prayers waiting to go into confession. Well, the young lad went into Father McCann's and was in ages before he re-appeared. He spent ages at the altar rail saying his penance and left.

In the meantime one of the old ladies had gone outside to the toilet and on her way back into church saw the young lad doing two somersaults and a back flip on the churchyard. She ran back into church and warned her friends to give confession a miss this week because she'd just seen what Father McCann was giving for his penance. This was one of Father McCann's own jokes and he must have told us it twenty times, but it always made us laugh.

And, 'Why does the Pope wear his underpants in the bath?'

'Because it's a sin to look down on the unemployed'.

I don't think that was one of Father McCann's. I think it was one of Rory Quiggley's.

10
THE LEGION OF MARY

As if we didn't get enough religious instruction, we had the Legion of Mary.

It had been started by Lilly Keenan in the early 1930s. She had gone to a Catholic teaching college and heard of the Legion through a colleague. Lilly taught at St Mary's School. The Legion had its origins in Dublin (wouldn't you know) and consisted of three sections: The Seniors - meeting on Thursday evenings; the Intermediaries - meeting on Friday evenings, and the Juniors - meeting on Saturday afternoons.

The meetings were held in the room above the playroom in St Mary's School, which smelt of dust and candles mixed with foisty dampness. It was almost oppressive, which somehow enhanced the atmosphere.

Our president was Mrs O'Hagan, who lived in the old priory next to the school, with her two daughters, Anne and Pat, and her mother and father. She was really kind and funny, unlike some of our schoolteachers.

The room had a long table with lots of chairs round it (it could probably seat thirty or forty people), an altar with a statue of Our Lady of Lourdes which was reputed to have come from Ireland. It was missing some fingers which had been poorly repaired. In the centre of the table was a strange looking object called a Vescillium, which represented the Holy Ghost.

The Holy Ghost was the third person of the blessed Trinity and was always present amongst us. We could pray and feel the presence of the Holy Ghost at any time. The Vescillium was like a miniature version of a Roman Legion standard or banner and had the eagle's wings outstretched on top of the 'Legio Mariae' logo in a square on top of the image of Our Lady with arms outstretched; all mounted on a marble ball and base plate. It was about eighteen inches high and had to be present on the table or the altar at every meeting.

The Legion of Mary was inspired by the Roman Legions who had undying loyalty to Rome, so the Legion of Mary had undying devotion to Our Lady. Its purpose was to further our knowledge of the faith and to manifest our devotion to Our Lady in prayer and to take home with us the high spiritual feeling created during the meeting which consisted of the Opening Prayer, the 'Our Father', the 'Hail Mary', and the Legion's Prayer:

In the name of the Father and of the son and of the Holy Ghost,
Fill the hearts of thy faithful and rekindle in them the force of thy love.
Send forth thy spirit and they shall be created and
Thou shalt renew the face of the earth.

Then the 'Allocutio', which was the address given by either the priest or the president and was always an instruction from the Hand Book which laid down the purpose of the Legion of Mary and the rules and requirements of members.

Then the secret bag collection, into which you put any spare coppers you happen to have with you. This was followed by the Magnificat.

My soul doth magnify the Lord and my spirit has rejoiced in God my Saviour, etc.

Then some talk about Our Lady's life and her involvement with her son, Jesus, and the importance of her position as intermediary to God. Then the Concluding Prayer:

We fly to thy patronage O Holy Mother of God,
Despise not our prayers in our necessities,
But ever deliver us from all dangers,
O glorious and blessed Virgin.
In the name of the Father and the Son and of the Holy Ghost.
Amen.
(Making the sign of the cross with the right hand)

The room was destroyed by a fire in the 1960s and only the glass eyes of Our Lady's statue were salvaged from the wreckage. Some people thought that was significant. Actually it has to be said that Cleator and Cleator Moor people were very superstitious. It was an Irish thing left over from the old Irish traditions which were against mainstream Catholic teachings, and peculiar to our part of West Cumberland. 'Little Ireland' at its best.

Superstitions

-If a black cat crossed your path you were going to have an accident and you stayed in doors for the rest of the day.

-Two crows landing on the fence together meant a death in the family.

-If you spilt salt you had to throw some over your left shoulder (or was it your right shoulder?) or you would be in for bad luck.

-Breaking a mirror meant seven years' bad luck.

-You never walked under a ladder. (I would imagine that was the most sensible of the lot, just in case you did get a bucket of distemper over your head.)

-If your feet were itchy you were going on a long journey.

-If the palm of your hand was itchy you were going to a wedding.

-If your ears were burning you were being talked about.

The same people were also very big on praying to certain saints, e.g.

-St Christopher - for a safe journey

-St Joseph - if you were unemployed and wanted work

-St Anthony - if you had lost something

-St Jude - for hopeless cases.

I'd opt for St Jude anytime. Just miss out the middleman and go straight to St Jude.

I wouldn't like to be a saint; the poor souls have terrible lives on earth with people stoning them to death or torturing them, and just when they think they're out of their misery and departed from this earth to their well deserved eternal rest, they're at every sinner's beck and call and getting pestered from all and sundry for favours. Although, of course, they do say, there's no rest for the wicked. None for saints either, I should think.

Holy Water was used like a voodoo spell by many. It was more popular than penicillin. Its use ranged from the care of chilblains to the prevention of multiple births. You just rubbed it onto the affected area and hoped for the best. Strangely enough it often worked. Another one of the Sacred Mysteries.

When the Grotto was completed in the late 1920s the Bishop was aware of the 'Cleator Moor Thing', and was against any further statues being erected in the grounds, because he was not too keen on the graven images getting out of control.

However, he was persuaded to allow a small Grotto and statue dedicated to St Teresa of the Roses, also known as the 'Little Flower' statue. It was a copy of the same shrine built in Carfin in Paisley, Scotland and was a very popular saint in the early 1930s.

LITTLE IRELAND

The Bishop said, 'That is it.' He didn't want the Grotto turned into a circus. 'No more statues.'

So it was to remain as it was until time immemorial. A place of prayer and pilgrimage and a very beautiful place to sit and reflect and enjoy the wonderful views of Dent Mountain, together with the peace and quiet of the Grotto grounds.

II
THE YOUNG MEN'S SOCIETY

We also had the Young Men's Society which was made up of lay members of the church who visited your house with a three-sectional photograph of Our Lady which they left at each household for a full week. They would then return and retrieve the picture.

They would arrive about ten men strong, say the Rosary in the living room in front of the picture with all the family present and request you to say your daily devotions to Our Lady every night in front of the picture, which had to be left in a prominent position until they returned the following week.

Mam would light a candle each night before we went to bed and we'd all say the Rosary together. The slogan was, 'The family who pray together stay together'. This seems like a very simplistic idea, but people genuinely believed in the family unit and saying your prayers together was as normal as having a meal together. We all willingly took part and felt well blessed for that very special week.

12
THE SACRED MYSTERIES

We have the Sacred Mysteries in the Catholic Church; these mysteries could not and should not be explained.

God gave us a brain, but we were told we could not understand all God's ways and should just accept them as truth without any question.

The Immaculate Conception and Transubstantiation were two of these mysteries.

The main difference between the Catholic and Protestant priests proclaimed by the Catholic Church was that the Catholic priest had the divine power through the sacrament of ordination, to change the bread and wine on the altar during the consecration into the physical body and blood of Jesus Christ. This is known as 'transubstantiation'. There was an unbroken line from Peter, the first Pope who authorised, through the Bishops, the full ordination of the priest according to Canon Law.

After the Reformation and the Dissolution of the Monasteries by Henry VIII, replacing the Roman Church with the Church of England. The Roman Church did not recognise the authority of Henry VIII as head of the Church of England to authorise ordination because the line was broken from that time and this difference was rigorously taught to us in school.

Looking down on Protestant vicars as usurpers who were not empowered to give the sacraments. This much-taught doctrine was taken by many Catholics in the 1950s to mean Protestants were the enemy of Catholics and they should not fraternise with them. Romantic relationships between Catholics and Protestants were not encouraged if not down-right forbidden by many families.

Catholics believe that Jesus was conceived by the Holy Ghost when he came down on Mary and planted his seed. So Jesus has no earthly Father. This was known as 'The Immaculate Conception'.

One of the sacred mysteries, or at least I think it must be a sacred mystery because whenever I asked for any information on it I was told, 'You'll find out when you're older and not to keep mithering', was where babbies came from.

LITTLE IRELAND

We had the stork theory, but I'd never seen a stork at Cleator or a rhubarb leaf big enough to hide a babby under. Then there was Stephen's theory that they came from rabbits' bellies.

I wasn't sure about that. I thought it could be something to do with women's bellies though, because as soon as we heard the whispers of, 'She's nursing again, I see, and she's still going out, you know'; 'Our Winnie saw her in the Co-op, as big as a house-end'; 'They've no shame going round in the daytime like that.' Well, I knew that 'like that' meant with a big belly.

So, I think babbies come from women's bellies. I don't for the life of me know how they get out mind you, but if it's one of the sacred mysteries, then we don't need to know. So long as they land on the pillow during the night so that the mother doesn't roll over and squash them in her sleep.

Another one of the sacred mysteries is how my Dad can go out for a couple of pints and come back blind drunk, or so my mother says, and 'going on the drink' is different to 'going for a few pints'.

I think going on the drink is when Dad comes in from the pub and starts talking daft. Mam'll say, 'I can't stand your daft talk, so I'm going to bed, Jay'.

He'll try to persuade her to stay and have a wee laugh, and she once said, 'Kiss my arse, Jay,' and left the room in a huff.

There's a song on the wireless by Doris Day called 'Que Sera, Sera', but the reception on our wireless is not always clear. It sort of comes and goes a bit and I thought she was singing 'Kiss my arse, my arse', so she must be mad with her boyfriend, although she doesn't sound as if she is. It must be another one of the sacred mysteries!

Protestants use different words to Catholics and they say them in a different way. Where we would say 'I'm going home', they say 'As goin yam.' They say 'larl', for small or wee, as we would say, and they use old-fashioned words like 'thou' and 'thine'. For 'How are you doing?', they say 'How's the gain on?' For 'I'm not feeling very good', they say 'Na as only moderate', or even 'As gay badly', which means I'm much worse than only moderate. 'What sec a fettle' is another. This means 'How are you keeping?'

They have names like Nathan Stanborough, Sep Todd, Ike Pool, Jim Pettie and Orial Steel. You know straight way they're Protestants. The Catholics use phrases like, 'Glory be to God and his Virgin Mother'

LITTLE IRELAND

and 'Jesus Christ, you'd try the patience of a Saint.' You'd never hear a Protestant say anything like that. The old Catholic women are always praying to 'Dear God' and his 'Sacred Mother' for somebody's safe deliverance. They have names like Pat Murphy, Eddie Devoy, John McCumiskey, Mary McAteer, Paddy O'Riley, Martha Kelly, Charlie Riley and Paddy Sheean.

Those last three must have had something to do with the sacred mysteries. Martha Kelly wore funny hats because she had no hair. Charlie Riley had no legs. He used to shuffle around on a wee bogey or would just lift himself forward on his hands as if his arms were crutches, and Paddy Sheean, well, I couldn't understand a word he said. One night I heard him ordering his food in the chip shop on Cleator Moor Square. It went something like 'PA..A..TIC HAP..A..TISH. PEA. A.. V..IC..OT.' This was instantly translated by May Fitzgerald as 'A penn'orth of fish, a ha'porth of chips and plenty of vinegar on, Paddy coming up'. Brilliant. Another sacred mystery.

13
KEIRHARDY AVENUE

Sometimes after our bath on a Saturday evening at Nana and Papa's house, Mam would say to me, 'How do you fancy sleeping here tonight? Nana and Papa will take you to eleven o'clock Mass in the morning, and you can stay until Benediction time then they'll drop you off on their way to chapel.'

I always felt half excited about the idea and wanted to seem keen for Mam's sake because it was obvious that that was what she wanted me to do.

It was always me because our Barry and Stephen wouldn't have stayed. Mam said Barry would be at Molly and Tony Hannah's tomorrow all day, and Stephen wouldn't leave her side even for one night, and she could do with a bit of a rest.

Our Margaret was no bother, she just played with her dolls or read a book or pottered about. Stephen was alright on his own as long as Mam was there. I was a bit of a live wire, I couldn't sit still, I agitated everyone one way or another, '...and I'll tell Nana to let you out to play with the lads on Keirhardy.'

That's where Nana and Papa lived, 26 Keirhardy Avenue. There was the number '26' on the front garden gate in little chrome numbers. The garden was well cared for by Papa. Nice lawns and a big hydrangea in the middle of the front lawn. He wasn't a fancy gardener, but he kept it neat and tidy, just like the house inside. It was a four-bedroomed Council house with a flat concrete roof. It had been built in the 1940s when there was a shortage of timber due to the war.

Inside it was like a little palace. There was always a smell of polish and you could have run your finger over any surface and would never have found a speck of dust. That was Aunty May's department, she lived with them. Her husband had gone to seek his fortune in America before the war. The plan was that he would get a job and a house and then send for Aunty May and the two children, Lilly and Jimmy. But for reasons best known to herself, she never followed him to America. Instead, she spent the rest of her life keeping house for Nana and Papa and bringing up her family and her grandchildren.

Cleaning and swilling the paths was her obsession. Cleaning the windows ran a close second.

It was a bit of a ritual this stop over, because they were old - at least Nana and Papa were; Aunty May was always full of beans. She'd put me to sleep in the double bed in the spare room. There was only one spare room because Nana and Papa had a bedroom each and Aunty May had her own room. The bed seemed to be three feet off the ground and it had a bolster and loads of pillows. She put my clothes for Mass in the morning on the chair by the bed and bid me goodnight. 'They were going to listen to the wireless for a wee while, but they'd be up directly so be a good lad and go to sleep.' No goodnight kiss. I was too big for all that carry on.

I was supposed to have a lie-in the following morning because there was plenty of time for a good breakfast before eleven o'clock Mass. I don't know why I needed to lie in because they were all up at sparrow fart. I suppose I'd just be in the way.

Papa used to clean his car on Sunday mornings and I would go with him to the garage site to fetch the car up to the house and all the local children would follow us and pester Papa for a ride back up the Avenue. He loved children and was always giving them coppers and taking a rise out of them in fun.

We always ended up with a car full, shouting and waving out of the car windows. Papa loved to have a crowd of children with him. Nana gave him a right dressing down when we arrived outside number 26, with the car heaving with all the waifs and strays of the day.

I heard her say, 'Stephen make that your finish. You'll have to stop taking kids in that car. What if anything happened to them? They could fall out and besides, people could get the wrong impression, you giving them coppers and rides in the car. Now I want you to stop it.'

'Oh, Good Christ, May Lizzy, is the world in such a state as to see badness in me giving the poor wee buggers a few coppers and a ride up the road in the car?'

'Yes it is Stephen. You read all sorts in the papers these days. Now I want you to stop it. Do you hear me? Give no-one any cause to talk, do you hear me?'

'I don't know, that beats cock fighting. It's a terrible state when you

LITTLE IRELAND

have to consider what bad-minded people might say. Well I'll go to Hell,' said Papa.

The car was lathered with lots of soapy water and polished to a shine you could see yourself in. It was a black Austin A40 and it was his pride and joy, next to us that is! We could climb all over it after he'd washed it and brushed it out. He wasn't obsessed with it like Aunty May was with the paths though.

Eleven o'clock Mass was a long drawn out affair. It was sung Mass with all the Latin responses sung by the choir. The High Altar incense, the lot. Father McCann getting fatter by the hour, he could hardly get up the altar steps. After a visit to the Grotto and graveyard with a few prayers over Great Nana Tool and Aunty Maggie's graves we were back for Sunday lunch. It was roast beef with Yorkshire pudding and loads of vegetables. Just water or lemonade to drink and a rice pudding for sweet.

The next part of the day was the biggest drag for me because Nana, Papa and Aunty May always took a siesta on Sunday afternoons. After they were all washed up and Papa had read the paper and had had his pipe at about three o'clock they all made their way upstairs and I was expected to go to bed as well.

Like I said earlier, I was the liveliest one of our family and how Aunty May persuaded me to take my clothes off and get into bed for an hour on a Sunday afternoon, God only knows! Mind you, anyone who knew Aunty May could believe it, because she was a very determined little woman. She would give it to me straight.

'You're going to bed for an hour.'

You didn't argue. If I did make a little bit of a protest, she wouldn't want Nana and Papa to hear so she'd cajole me till she got me into the bedroom then say, 'Now come on just for an hour Sean. It'll be over before you can count to ten.'

She'd watch me get my clothes off, tuck me in and close the door gently behind her.

This particular afternoon I decided to make a run for it. I'd give them five minutes to settle down then I'd get dressed again and go down Kierhardy to the sweet shop at the bottom of the hill. It used to be a Methodist church, but two old men, twin brothers I think, who lived up the Fell Road, had made the front part into a sweet shop.

LITTLE IRELAND

They wore those cotton, shitty-brown coat-type overalls with long sleeves, they were both deaf as posts but were really nice. I once went in and asked for some mint balls and the one serving me said, 'I'm sorry lad, but I don't sell moth balls.'

When I said 'No, I said *mint* balls,' he said, 'I know. But I still don't sell moth balls.'

I settled for a quarter of humbugs and half expected him to say 'I don't sell handbags', but he didn't.

When I got to the wee shop it was closed and there I was with a load of coppers Papa had given me burning a hole in my pocket, and no shop open to spend them.

I'd sneaked down the stairs with my shoes in my hand and escaped by the back door which was bolted and barred like Fort Knox. As soon as I'd closed the door behind me, I put on my shoes and hopped it as fast as I could go. I'd planned to get my sweets and sit on the wall next to the telephone box and make my way back when I thought the hour was nearly up. They'd be none the wiser. I thought I could run up the Moor to the candy shop on the square. If I hurried it wouldn't take all that long.

Sunday was always a dead day on Cleator Moor. Everyone was either taking a siesta or in the pubs. I hardly passed a soul on Ennerdale Road, except for Agnes Burford, who always stood on her front step dressed up with her best coat and hat on and handbag over her arm, pretending she was going somewhere. She'd stand there for hours not making any attempt to move; just passing the time of day with anyone who would stop and chat. Most people knew better than to stop.

Nana used to say, 'Wouldn't you think she'd go and sit with her mother, she lives just a few doors down.'

But no, rain, hail or shine Agnes stood her ground. I suppose she wanted people to think she's got somewhere to go, the poor old lass.

You could hear them all shouting in the *Derby Arms* and I hoped Dad was not among them, or I'd be in trouble. I don't know though, he'd probably take me in for a shandy.

I don't believe this, the candy shop is closed as well. Wouldn't you think they'd stay open in case anyone wanted a holy statue? It was

LITTLE IRELAND

Sunday after all and it's the only shop on Cleator Moor that sells holy statues and rosary beads, as well as sweets.

I'd better get back so I'll take a shortcut through Fletcher Street, even though Aunty May says if you don't want nits and ringworm keep away from it. It's not that bad, a bit scruffy looking but it'll save me a bit of time and I'm running out of that.

About half way down Fletcher Street on the moor side, I see a light on in one of the parlour windows and then someone standing near the window. Bloody hell, I don't believe it. It's an old woman with no clothes on. True as God, she's standing just back from the window staring out and she's got long droopy breasts and a hairy pom-pom. She scared the shit out of me. I take off and run like hell till I get back to Kierhardy Avenue. Agnes Burford is still standing in her Sunday best when I pass and she says, 'Hello,' hoping I'm going to stop for the crack. No chance! I'm in enough trouble without being interrogated by her.

Aunty Bibby was coming out of her house just below Nana and Papa's house. She is really Great Aunty Bibby, Nana's twin sister - they look like two peas in a pod, but Aunty Bibby has a cockney accent. She had moved to London in her teens to get work and married a Londoner, Tommy Little. He was a policeman in London and she'd lived there for about 30 years. She and her children, Bobby, Tommy and Maisey, had been evacuated during the blitz. They came to live with Nana and Papa until they were fixed up with there own home. They decided not to return to London after the war because she was divorced from her husband and she had all her family in Cumbria.

Aunty Bibby was not like Nana in her ways. She was very distrusting of people, even her son Bobby, who she sometimes didn't even recognise. She came running into Nana's one afternoon and told her there was a strange man sitting in her living room and she wanted Nana to go with her and find out what he wanted. When they got to the house it was only Bobby, her own son and she still didn't recognise him. I wouldn't mind but Bobby lived with her!

Aunty Bibby often visited Nana, and it was a pantomime when she was going home because she never knew which was her house. Nana had to go to the garden gate with her and direct her to her own house.

She'd say, 'No Bridgett, it's past the front row here, then turn in and your house is straight in front of you at the end of the square.'

She still got confused and Nana would get her coat on and see her to her door - even then she wasn't fully convinced. She'd got to the stage where she'd go up the Moor for her shopping and people would walk her back home because she just didn't know where she was. Nana said she was found insisting she lived where the new police station was, close to the square, adamant her house was somewhere nearby.

The man who told Nana about her insistence had brought her back home in his car. Nana said they had lived in one of the cottages which was originally on the site the new police station occupied when they were children and she thought she still lived there. Because they had been pulled down years ago and the police station built on the same site, she was even further confused.

It's half past four by the kitchen clock and there's no sign of life. I quickly lock and double bolt the back door and race upstairs. The lock and bolts in Papa's house are always well oiled and greased as is everything else in the house. Dad says, 'If Stephen can't oil it, he'll creosote it,' because all the garden fences, coal house and shed are creosoted every year, sometimes twice a year. Dad said, 'They should last for a hundred years, the treatment they all get.'

You see Dad's not a man who looks after things. Mam says, 'He can never lay his hands on any of his tools when he wants them. Not like Papa who knows where everything is and looks after all his gear.'

I suppose that's because he had his own transport business, buses and taxis and spent most of his spare time stripping an engine or relining the brakes on one of his buses. He needed to know where everything was. Now he has only got the lawn mower and the doors to oil. Mind you, he does Aunty Winnie's, Aunty Lilly's and Mam's hinges and bolts. When he comes down to our house he often brings his oil can because he knows Dad doesn't bother oiling anything.

I've made it - only just in time. I jump on the bed and Aunty May shoves her face round the bedroom door and says, 'My God we've all slept in. I see you're up and dressed. Did you sleep then?'

I answer 'Yes I did, off and on.'

'That's a good lad. I told you, you would didn't I? I'm going down to put the kettle on for a cup of tea. I'll leave Nana and Papa until the tea is made. Mind they won't want to sleep all day. You come down stairs with me now.'

Just as we got into the kitchen and Aunty May lit the gas ring, there was a knock at the back door. It was wee Mary Dunn come to see Nana. They were cousins and both very fond of each other. Wee Mary had three of her own grandchildren with her, two girls and a boy.

They were not very old; the youngest only about three and the other girl and boy much of an age, about five and six, I suppose. They were like three wee urchins. Aunty May invited them in. She explained to wee Mary about oversleeping and that Nana will be up directly, so to go into the kitchen and she'd get her a cup of tea. She left to get Nana and Papa up.

Wee Mary said, 'Are you one of Eileen's lads?'

I said, 'Yes.'

'You'll be one of the twins, are ye?'

'That's right, I'm Sean.'

'Are you here on a wee visit lad?' she asked, and I said, 'Yes, I'm here to give my Mam a bit of a rest, but I'm going home tonight.'

'Aye, you'll be needing to be home for school in the morning, lad.'

The three urchins were starting to play up. The two oldest ones were poking each other and the wee three-year-old lay down on the floor and started to do a rollover on the cold lino.

'Will you all behave yourselves and don't be making a show of me in front of May Lizzy and May, now do yers hear me?' said wee Mary.

At this point the five-year-old girl hurled herself onto the floor and did a handstand. May and Nana walked into the room and wee Mary said, 'How are ye lass, you look well.'

Nana said, 'I'm doing nicely Mary thanks, how's yourself? Are these your John's kids?'

'Aye, I've took them to give their mother a bit of peace for an hour. They're a handful for her.'

Then wee Mary called out, 'Anne get back onto ye feet or I'll slap your arse for ye.'

LITTLE IRELAND

Well that would have been easy from where I was sitting because, to my horror, she had no knickers on and she was upside down with her frock round her head. Her pom-pom was at eye level with me. I didn't know where to put myself. This was the second pom-pom I had seen that day, only the second in my life in fact, and both in the same afternoon. Only hers was like a little peach where as the old woman's had a wee beard.

I wish to hell I could go home now. I've had enough.

'Would you look at the state of her May Lizzy, she's got no knickers on and right in front of that wee lad,' said wee Mary.

I just went redder and redder till Aunty May said, 'Why don't you and Billy go onto the square and play for a while Sean, and I'll give you a shout when I've got the tea ready.'

Billy was obviously used to seeing his sister's pom-pom because he didn't react but I wasn't; our Margaret was never seen naked in front of her brothers and vice versa. This was a big shock for me.

The rest of the day came and went without any further event. Nana and Papa dropped me off home at six o'clock after my tea, on their way to Benediction and everyone wanted to know what I'd been doing.

'Oh, this and that, nothing much. I don't think I want to stay on my own any more at Nana's, Mam, there's nothing to do', I said.

'Aye, well, you are getting a bit big for that now. I know they fuss a bit, so we'll see', said Mam.

I felt that was the last time I'd spend Sunday afternoon in bed, even though I hadn't been in bed. In fact, I was certain because I had made up my mind. As much as I loved them, I was not going through all that again.

John Cromwell, Dad's mate, had seen me from the *Commercial* window and told Dad I'd been wondering round the Moor on my own, and when Dad tackled me about it and I told him about being put to bed he went mad with Mam.

He said, 'That's the finish Eileen, they'll be making a 'Nancy' boy out of him, if we're not careful. Sending a lad to bed on a Sunday afternoon! I'm not surprised he went off on his own.'

Mam said, 'Aye, we'll say no more about it, Jay, and don't mention it to Mammy and Daddy, I want no falling out about it. He won't be staying on Sundays again', agreed Mam.

'He should be at home with his brothers, not cooped up with the old people. No wonder he took off', said Dad.

I felt as if that was well sorted now and I wouldn't have to run the gauntlet of Ennerdale Road and Fletcher Street again on Sundays, but it had been a Hell of a laugh when I told Stephen and Barry about the old woman on Fletcher Street and the upside down antics in Nana's back kitchen.

What a day!

14
BIRKS ROAD - RENATO SEGALINI

I had a penny for the Bishop's Fund, not a 'Cat in Hell's chance' of getting a red star. Mam gave us a few coppers every day and the deal was that we gave up sweets! We didn't have that many sweets to start with, but Penguins were off the menu after tea for the duration of Lent except for St Patrick's Day, when mid-way through we could indulge for a full day.

Susan McAvoy, Rory Quiggley and Paul Dunn were always in the running for the gold star; they brought half-crowns in each time and the week before the end of Lent the graph was going up like a thermometer in a heat wave. The idea was to collect as much money as possible by whatever means, preferably by self-denial or good deeds from Ash Wednesday until Good Friday. The money was donated to charities such as the Orphans' Fund and sick children's funds.

The donations were put onto a chart with the child's name beside each donation and some of the parents saw this as an opportunity to make a statement, and the child who donated the most money got to meet the Bishop and be presented with a gold star - very prestigious for the parents. It was usually the better off or one-child families. It was not really fair as there were four of us and collectively our combined donations were usually equal to, or sometimes exceeded, the top single donation, but as Mam says, 'Life isn't always fair and think of the poor wee orphans who would benefit'.

Nana Close and Nana Heron often gave us coppers for the Bishop's Fund and left instruction for us to say a decade of the Rosary or do a Novena to our Lady in return.

Aunty May was a keen devotee of the Bishop's Fund and was forever leaving envelopes with the odd sixpence and coppers in on a Sunday night for Mam to share out between us for the Monday morning class collection, the main one of the week.

Mr McCrickard was always at pains to point out that although it was a great honour to be presented with the gold star, every penny was important and the smallest donation was every bit as important as the biggest. He often picked out the person with the smallest donation and made a big thing out of asking how it had been collected and congratulated the donor for a very good effort.

That little reference to Aunty May just isn't enough. She was the oldest surviving sister of Mam, ten years older to be precise, and she can only be described as a 'one off.' Her daughter Lily, was ten years younger than Mam, and because Mam had her family late and Lily had had hers at a young age, her children were considered by us to be our cousins, being of a similar age as us. Although Lily was, in fact, our cousin, we thought of her as our lovely, kindly aunt. She loved children and showered us with affection and kindness.

If Mam would scold us, Aunty Lily would stop her and say, 'Leave them alone our Eileen, you have the best kids in the world there', and Mam would say, 'Aye, well, its because I'm always onto them that they are good kids, Lily. It doesn't happen by accident, you know'. She'd soften a bit towards us after making her point. A minor victory to Aunty Lily.

Aunty May loved hats, she was never without one; not used as a fashion statement, more a way of keeping her hair under control, I suspect. On cold wet days she would don her maroon coat and felt hat, covered by a translucent mackintosh and a concertina plastic rain hood. She always seemed to have too many clothes on. I don't know how she managed to walk.

She worked as a dinner-lady at St Pat's School and always called in on Lily on her way home from work, to check on her and the children. Lily seemed to always let her have her say even against her better judgement.

'Now, have you changed Raymond's bed today, Lily? I'll do it for you if you haven't lass'.

'Yes, Mammy, I've changed his bed and I've cleaned the windows and dusted as well'.

'Aye, well, I'll just go over the windows lass, I notice on my way in that you've missed a few wee bits.'

Sometimes Lily would protest, but more often than not she'd just give into her and let her get on with it. She would even let her wash her neck and knees when she decided that she could see dirt on them. She'd say, 'Our Lily's got that sallow skin and she never looks clean. I'll just give your neck and knees a good scrub lass, to be on the safe side'.

Lily would pull a face and sit on the kitchen coppy and let her get

LITTLE IRELAND

on with it, because it was easier than putting up a fight and listening to her go on about it for hours.

Aunty May had a knack of making you feel guilty if she asked you to do something and you didn't want to do it. She would say, 'My God, after all the things I do for you and our Eileen, and you won't even go a message for me once in a blue moon.'

It always worked with me. I was a pushover, but her grandson Raymond, wasn't on any such guilt trip with May, he would say, 'No Nanny, I'm not going,' and that would be her opening to put those moist, penetrating eyes on me and I couldn't say no. She'd send us to Maria Rudd's for a half-stone of tatties and we could get a lollipop from the change.

Maria wore bright red lipstick and red cheeks like a Kelly doll. She chased you if she thought you were taking a shortcut up the backs to the main street through her shop. It was a butcher shop with the big sides of beef and pigs' heads all on display with flies as big as hedgehogs hopping from one piece of meat to the next, nothing was ever refrigerated, but the ceiling hung with fly papers dangling like Chinese streamers, with a holocaust of the day's catch.

I was often farmed out to Aunty Lily's for the odd weekend, to play with my cousin Raymond and his younger brother Steven, wee Steven as he was known, a cherub-like blond, curly-haired bugger. Raymond wouldn't tolerate him for any longer than five minutes because he was spoiled by Aunty May and wanted his own way all the time and usually got it! He could sulk for Great Britain. I always wished I could sulk like him. I wasn't much of a sulker. I hated the unpleasantness it caused. But not wee Steven. He was highly skilled in that department and Raymond couldn't stand him.

Aunty May would say to me, 'Take wee Steven with you lad. Just for me and I'll give you some money for sweets, but keep an eye on him for God's sake because our Raymond won't. Here take these coppers and look after them do you hear? Good lad, now just for me'.

We'd set off for the slag bank, Raymond saying 'I'm not looking after him, Sean, he wants his own way all the time, so he's all yours'.

I'd then be left trying to keep the peace between the two of them and trying to enjoy myself at the same time.

Raymond wet the bed, and I slept in the same bed as him and wasn't used to sleeping on a rubber sheet. Raymond's Dad, John, had

LITTLE IRELAND

a yellow plastic belt hanging up on a hook behind the kitchen door and he used to say to us on the way up the stairs, 'No carry on out of you two, or you'll get the belt.'

The constant presence of the belt and the reminder on the way up the stairs kept us on our best behaviour. That being said, I loved my weekends at Birks Road except if it rained on the Saturday afternoon and we were stuck in the house, because Uncle John listened to the football results on the wireless for what seemed like hours, and we couldn't make a noise in case he missed a draw. That was when my mind would wander to being at home and never having to be quiet because we had a big attic and could make as much noise as we liked up there and no-one ever complained.

Aunty Lily would fuss round us and say it won't be long now lads, just keep quiet for a wee while longer and we'll have our tea. I'll make you some salmon and chips, nice brown chips the way you all like them. Raymond and I would look at each other and enthuse in a silent sort of way.

About that time there had been a small influx of foreign immigrants. Some Czechs, Yugoslavs, Poles and Italians came to Cleator Moor, mainly Italians and in fact they all seemed to be living in and around North Street and Aldby Street.

You could tell the Italian houses at Christmas time because they all devoted the whole of their front downstairs windows to the Christmas Story, each one depicting the infant Jesus with the Wise Men and the Shepherds. Not just a little crib on a window sill, you got the whole works laid out on a table with a black sheet draped at the back of the table and fixed to the top of the curtain pole to act as a back drop.

This would be dotted with stars and the bright star from the east was a white Christmas tree light permanently lit up to guide the Wise Men. They were very inventive with their tableaux. Cecil B De Mille couldn't have done better, in fact they gave the locals the idea and they followed suit by fixing Christmas tree lights all round the perimeter of their windows and dropped the religious theme altogether.

My first Italian friend was Renato Segalini. We first saw him skulking round the monkey bars at the playing field. He looked foreign with his slicked-back hair and his olive skin. He could say a few English words but was determined to learn more from us.

LITTLE IRELAND

Raymond said, 'He's one of the *'Eyeties'* from Aldby Street. Should we see if he wants to play?'

He did want to play, and we communicated with the enthusiasm of young lads wanting to get to know each other and to impress each other with their dexterity and sporting skills. Renato was stocky and couldn't get across the monkey bars in one go, so we were able to display our superior skills and encourage him to follow. Within a few days we could have a proper conversation - all down to Renato's grasp of the Cleator Moor, Irish/English. God help him, no-one else in the world would be able to understand a word he said.

Renato insisted one afternoon that we go with him to meet his Mama, and we couldn't dissuade him. We arrived at the front door and he said in his own way that his Mama wanted to meet his friends. As soon as he opened the door the foreignness was immediately obvious by the lack of carpets and the smell of something I had never smelt before, like strong onions and bad fish; it turned out to be garlic.

Mrs Segalini was a proper Italian Mama; all round and noisy, making huge gestures with her hands and holding our faces and saying things like 'Mama Mia' and 'Bella, Bella'. She couldn't say a single word of English.

After the initial introduction from Renato, and Mrs Segalini repeating 'Sean' and 'Raymond', and laughing like a drain, we were gestured to sit down at the table. It was laid with a heavy woven cloth, which looked like a horse blanket, and some soup bowls. She turned to Renato with a totally different tone of voice, as if she was about to kill him, and screamed some instructions to him, before turning back to us with an expression on her face like the statue of the Little Flower.

She spoke very gently to us in Italian for at least five minutes, clearly expecting a response. When she didn't get one, she screamed at Renato again at about a hundred-miles-an-hour. He came back to the table and somehow explained that his mother had love for us and we had to stay for tea, or the Italian equivalent. My mother used to say I would eat 'shit with sugar on', but this was going to be the acid test. Shit with sugar on was one thing, but spaghetti and meatballs was a totally different ball game.

Renato started to serve the said *'cibo'* (Italian word for food) and the long white strings or worms piled onto our plates. I didn't know whether to stab it with my fork, or run like hell. Instead, I just sat in a state of panic and hoped the table would collapse, or someone would drop dead, to save me from having to refuse it, as it was obvious even to a wee lad that that would have caused great office. However, I needn't have worried about the spaghetti, as the meatballs were even worse. They did look like shit with sugar on. Mrs Segalini gestured to us to start eating and verbally abused Renato again for several minutes, until he finally sat down at the table.

Raymond looked at me and I looked at him, unable to give him any reassurance. But I held my breath, took the knife and fork in my hands and proceeded to poke the mess on the plate. Mrs Segalini erupted again to Renato and smiled her saintly smile at us. While Renato took his spoon and fork, plaited the spaghetti round his fork using the spoon as an anchor and had a huge walnut whip of a thing pushing into his mouth in seconds.

'That was how you did it,' said the expression on Mrs Segalini's face.

Well, believe it or not, I managed a couple of dozen strands onto my fork and clumsily spun them onto the spoon and up to my mouth. Mrs Segalini's eyes were 'out on her cheeks', and her gaze was fixed firmly on my mouth. I had to do it, in it went. I braced myself and stopped breathing while the white soft tapeworms wriggled in my mouth. She held her gaze and sat motionless while I swallowed. I got the surprise of my life. It tasted mostly of nothing - just a hint of tomato and some other flavour I didn't recognise, but not unpleasant. I was nearly there, just the meatballs to go. God help me.

By this time Raymond had finished his first mouthful and was starting on his next with enthusiasm. Mrs Segalini was wetting herself with delight and Renato had the first smile on his face I'd seen since we met. The meatballs were soft and spicy and rather strong for my taste, being used to my mother's beef teas and roast dinners, but again not unpleasant. The spaghetti was growing on my plate, it seemed the more I ate the more was on the plate.

After about half an hour of solid slog, I finished the lot and was given a glass of watered down red wine to wash it down. It tasted like altar wine, so it wasn't quite so alien to me. I even managed that. I felt as if I'd had a monumental experience from another planet.

As soon as we finished, Renato cleared the table whilst his mother came round and kissed us both on the cheeks. She held our faces and gazed at us and babbled non-stop in quiet tones and then fired into Renato again. On his return to the table she threw her arms round him and kissed him with a vengeance and held onto our hands and went from one to another of us gesturing at the table and then to us. Renato said, 'Mama, she like you. You eat Italian tea with us again.'

His mama then disappeared into the kitchen howling in tears and incantations. I was shell-shocked and as full as a fitch.

When we went home to Raymond's, Aunty May gave us hell for being late. The table was laid and the beans and chips already on the plates going cold.

Raymond said, 'You needn't have bothered Nanny, we've had our teas.'

'What do you mean you've had your teas? Where have you had your teas?'

'At Renato's.'

'You mean you've had your teas at the Italian's house?'

'Yes.'

Surprisingly she was not all that angry, more curious. She said, 'My God, what did you have to eat?' and when we said 'Spaghetti and meat balls,' she nearly passed out, 'Mother of God, you could have been poisoned.'

Aunty Lily on the other hand was very calm and obviously amused by our innocent admission, she said, 'And did you eat it lads?' to which we replied, 'Yes and it was nice.' Aunty Lily was trying to hold back the laughing and looking at the shocked expression on Aunty May's face at the same time. Eventually she composed herself and said, 'Well isn't that nice of Mrs Segalini, you'll have to bring Renato over here for his tea one night after school. I can't get over you eating spaghetti. I couldn't eat it to save my life.'

I could hear Aunty May saying to Aunty Lily, 'Do you think they'll be alright? Maybe we should give them some salty water to make them sick, Lily.'

Aunty Lily just kept laughing and saying, 'No Mammy, they're alright. The wee buggers, fancy them eating spaghetti, I can't get over it. Wait till I tell our Eileen.'

One infamous Saturday afternoon after playing on the monkey bars for an hour and teaching Renato the rudiments of tennis and partnering him, showing him how to hit the ball with the racquet. The job became too laborious for Raymond and me, we couldn't get into our usual frenzy with each other, so we were resting in the long grass at the edge of the tennis court when in the middle distance we were suddenly aware of a clutch of lasses.

Raymond said, 'Oh Hell, its Carol Toomey and them twins. Just pretend you haven't seen them.'

It wasn't easy to pretend you couldn't see them because they started to circle round us, like a team of sheep dogs rounding on the sheep. They weren't playing the way most lasses played. They were more like lads playing loper kitty or British bulldog. The twins took it in turn to be swung round by the legs and hurled into the long soft grass by Carol, who was a bit bigger than them and although slight in build, as strong as a horse.

They weren't giggly like other lasses either; they were rough and predatory in their behaviour. We pretended not to notice them and they didn't like it.

Carol, who had long black, curly hair and was like Gypsy Rose Lee and behaved like Carmen Miranda without the bananas, approached us and asked, 'What are you lot looking at?'

Well, that was a stupid question, because what the hell else could we be looking at when what looked like the dance of the seven veils was being thrust at us from spitting distance?

We didn't answer her, which seemed to infuriate her even more.

She then said, 'What do you lot think you're looking at? Are you deaf or something?'

Raymond now replied, 'We might be deaf, but we're not daft, so piss off and leave us alone.'

Carol was amused by this and plonked herself down in the middle of us. She looked me straight in the eye and said, 'What do they call him?' directing her question to Raymond, who said, 'Sean. Why?'

'I'm just asking,' she replied, and looked me up and down in the way they do on cowboy films just before they spit their tobacco out and shoot the sheriff. She then dismissed me and shot round and pushed her face into Renato's and said, 'Who's this then?' and went even closer to him and hissed at him, 'Can you not talk either?'

Renato was even more shocked than me and turned his head away. She seemed as if she was about to pounce on him when Raymond said, 'I thought I told you to piss off, Toomey?'

This was too much for her so she hurled herself onto Raymond and started to thump him with the strength and style of a trained boxer. Raymond restrained her and rolled on top of her, keeping her hands firmly fixed onto the grass with his knees. She was shouting and kicking like a good'un, and Raymond was looking at her and saying, 'Well, Toomey who's the big shot now? Why don't you get up and give me a good hiding? Go on let's see if you can.'

Carol spat straight into his face, and he let her go calling her a 'dirty wee bitch'.

Suddenly her mood changed, she moved away from us slightly and beckoned the twins over to join her.

You've heard the expression 'A bulldog chewing a wasp?' Well, that's just what they looked like. A 'slapped arse', a 'chicken looking down a spout', a 'stopped clock', a 'face like bad fat', any of these expressions was appropriate. They were dogs!

One of the twins pounced on me and grabbed my hand and said, 'Gonna arm wrestle Shone, Shone, Shone?'

And while you could cough, she had my arm flat on the ground. I hadn't had a chance to prepare myself.

I shot up and said, 'Come on then do it properly this time,' and she said 'Oh, do it properly this time, do it properly this time, hark at him!' And with that she moved away from me to Renato who jumped up and started to walk away.

She stood up and said, 'Big shit, big shit, big shit.' Why she needed to repeat herself so much was a mystery to me, she seemed to have come from another planet. Then she started to chant, 'Tell tale tit, your mother can't knit, your father can't walk with a walking stick.'

This was a pointless exercise because poor Renato couldn't understand a word she was saying, but he knew he'd better butt out or he'd end up hitting one of them, and he knew he shouldn't do that. Raymond shouted him back and he returned once he realised they were also retreating.

When they arrived they had been sucking lollipops and one of the twins had kept her stick in her hand. The quieter one that was, she was absolutely identical to the parrot of a sister of hers. Carol floated off over the playing field wall and disappeared and left the ugly twins to flatten some more long grass and make more unearthly noises as they gradually settled down some yards away from us to whisper and make jibes at us from a safe distance (safe for us that is!).

We decided to go back to Raymond's, leave our tennis racquets in the house and take Renato to the slag bank and catch some newts and a bit of peace and quiet after being assaulted by the 'Witch of Nannycatch' and her assailants.

Aunty May homed in right away when she saw me. She had a sixth sense about these things, 'What's the matter lad, you look as if you've seen a ghost?'

Raymond answered for me, 'No Nanny, nothing as nice as a ghost, he's just had ten rounds with Carol Toomey and the grudge twins'.

'My God' said Aunty May, 'What have I told you Raymond about them lasses? You want nowt to do with them. Do you hear me?'

Poor Raymond replied, 'Nanny as soon as they see somebody new, they're over to see if they can frighten them, but we saw them off, didn't we Sean?'

'Aye, well give them a wide berth from now on, do you hear me? You'll be glad to get back home lad when your mother comes for you tonight, after being with these mad buggers up here,' and laughed a raucous laugh.

15
YELLOW JAUNDICE

The two sandstone slabs that form the roof of the outside lavatory to our house make a great vantage point from which to view the street life, and there's loads of that.

I've got yellow jaundice and my Mam told Nana Heron that I'm as yellow as a duck's foot, and my face is like a piece of finney haddy. That's just what I felt like, to eat that is, a lovely bit of finney haddy and a big knob of butter. I must be feeling better when I'm thinking of food, for days I haven't eaten a bite. My Mam is bound to have finney haddy, or if she hasn't, she'll go and get some for me, because she'll do anything for us, when we're not well.

We'll be going to Nana's and Papa's tonight for our bath, we haven't got a bathroom. We've got a tin bath and until lately Mam used to fill it from the gas boiler in the kitchen and put it in front of the fire in the living-room and we'd all get a bath together, Barry Stephen and me, and when we'd finished Margaret would have her bath and then Mam, usually with the original water, unless we'd been really dirty, then Mam would empty the bath with pans and refill it.

So going to Papa Heron's was much easier for her and we enjoyed the occasion, because Papa Heron and Nana were great fun, especially Papa, who would duck us under the water and splash us and roar with laughter.

Papa told Mam last week that my dry skin needed his special treatment. I'm looking down at my knees, they're all wrinkled and my hands are like an old man's hands. Mind you Papa's treatment has made my skin much better, it doesn't feel so dry and sore as it used to, so last Saturday Papa started his skincare programme.

First of all, a light dry down after my bath, which had Dettol in it. Mind you it could be worse because Papa puts Jeyes Fluid in his own bath, maybe that's why he always looks so pink.

Then he thickened me all over with Vaseline and told Nana to go and get some clouts to wrap around my knees and ankles. He piled the Vaseline on my worst areas, knees and ankles and bound them with the clouts. I looked like an Egyptian mummy. I walked into the living room and went straight to Nana for a bit of comfort.

LITTLE IRELAND

She said, 'Oh, God help you, you poor wee thing.' That did the trick.

Auntie May said, 'He loves to be badly doesn't he?' and I was shocked, from that day on I'm never going to give the impression I like being badly.

Auntie May said to Mam, 'If he gets kins, make him pee into a jug and bathe his fingers in it, that's the best cure. Mind it has to be his own pee.'

Thank God for that, I had visions of me being sent to Joe Farren's hut, with my jug and shove it under his lurcher bitch, and then have to sink my mitts into that. Can you imagine the smell, not to mention the taste when I forgot and started to bite my nails?

Mam has had her instructions from Papa, 'Eileen you must remember to thicken his knees and ankles every night and bind them with the clouts before he goes to bed. If he sleeps in them for a couple of weeks, he'll be much better, the poor wee bugger.' I'm sure his eyes filled up as he handed me over to Mam.

So Papa's skin cure treatment was working, or maybe that's why I've got yellow jaundice, something to do with the Vaseline, it's a bit yellow you know, maybe I've overdosed on Vaseline. Well, whatever.

The sun is shining, I've been off school all week and the lasses are gathering for a game of skipping. Ada Kelly and Emily Flemming are having a crack leaning against Ada's yard gate, putting the world to rights I suppose. I can't hear them very well, I can just make out Ada saying, 'They're real bad lads you know' and Emily saying, 'Well, they couldn't be anything else, look at the Father, he was no good.'

'Aye well its in them what ails them, as the saying goes,' says Ada, with much mouth setting and bust lifting. I wonder who they're talking about. Blast they've gone in, I'll never get to know now.

Mary Stones and Elsie Eccles had the rope, it's about eleven foot long and the longer the rope the more difficult it is to skip with, something to do with timing and rhythm.

Roseline McAteer is first into the rope followed swiftly by my cousin Maureen Devoy and Ann McAteer so that's three of them all keeping perfect time with the rope. The two turners are highly skilled at keeping the rope evenly taut and turning at the same pace.

A HOUSE TO LET APPLY WITHIN

WHEN I GO OUT EILEEN KELLY COMES IN

LITTLE IRELAND

Eileen Kelly promptly replaces Ann McAteer and the rhythm continues, skip after skip after skip of perfect timing. It's incredible to watch and I'm in the perfect position for it. The pace of the skipping is getting gradually faster and Maureen Devoy starts to chant.

A HOUSE TO LET APPLY WITHIN

WHEN I GO OUT ELSIE ECCLES COMES IN

Elsie dives in like something from Billy Smart's Circus and the pace is getting faster and faster. Mary Stones tells Maureen Devoy to do 'A house to let' so she can have a go. So she starts,

A HOUSE TO LET APPLY WITHIN

WHEN I GO OUT MARY STONES COMES IN

Mary's like a trampoline artist and can jump up on one leg and land on the other and still keep to the rhythm and timing perfectly.

I can see Uncle Faley further up the backs sitting on his wooden copy, watching the world go by. He lives with Auntie Winnie and Uncle Eddie Devoy, in fact he's Auntie Winnie's uncle and my great-uncle, Nana Heron's brother. He's a bachelor and lives most of his life with my grandmother, but for some reason he's living with Auntie Winnie now, and I think he's a mixed blessing to her.

She says if he doesn't change his drawers more often she's going to refuse to wash them. 'He's a dirty old bugger,' she says. He's retired from the pit now and spends most of his days moaning about the price of razor blades from Miles Bawden's. Auntie Winnie says, 'He'll go on the bus to Cleator Moor rather than pay four pence for a razor blade from Miles. He can buy them for three pence from the Moor, and it costs him sixpence for his bus fare. Now where's the sense in that?'

She was raging the other day because she asked him to paint the mangle in the back yard while she was up the Moor shopping, just to give him something to do. When she left him he was looking for a paint brush, but when she got back two hours later she could hear a load of banging coming from up the stairs. When she went up shouting 'Faley is that you?'

He said, 'Aye lass, I'm up on the attic stairs.'

When she found him he was struggling near the top of the attic stairs with the mangle which weighed a ton, and when she said 'What are you doing Faley?' he said 'I'm going to paint the mangle when I get it on to the attic.'

LITTLE IRELAND

She said, 'What's wrong with painting it in the yard?' and he said 'Well, I wasn't going to trail all the way up here for the paint brush and back down again, so I brought the mangle with me.'

She called him all the dopey old so and so's she could lay her tongue to and he says, 'Bejesus Winnie, I can't do right for doing wrong for you these days. What's wrong with you?'

'What's wrong with me?' she asked. 'Wouldn't it have been far easier for you to get the paint brushes and take them down to the yard, than trail this bloody thing up here?'

'Oh, well, I never thought of that now Winnie,' said Faley.

He wasn't the brightest of men old Faley, but his heart was in the right place. Winnie says 'He'll do anything for you, but the trouble is he can't do anything.'

He was second generation Irish and he was 'As Irish as the pigs in Dublin' to listen to him. Actually, he'd never been on Irish soil.

Winnie said he's been telling everybody he's nearly done his back in painting the mangle. He's got her demented.

The lasses are doing 'peppers' by now.

HIGH LOW DOLLY PEPPER

ONE, TWO, THREE

The rope's going ninety-miles-an-hour. I can hardly see it, it's going so fast, and Elsie's going purple in the face, but she's not going to stop. Roselyn McAteer bad foots it and catches the rope on its way up. She tries to right herself, but ends up falling flat on her face on the concrete. Everybody rushes to pick her up, she's a bit stunned but she's not bleeding, so she's shoved to one side and the game starts all over again without her. It's the survival of the fittest this skipping game. I'm glad I'm just watching.

Well, this yellow jaundice is alright, but I can't bear sitting around for a long time, so if Mam's not watching I'll get my bogey out and go and see if my cousin Robert Looney is coming out to play. Robert lives just up the backs from us on Main Street, his Mam, Auntie Margaret, is Dad's sister. Robert had two sisters, Alice and Carmel and a brother Christopher.

Our Stephen and me have recently discovered that we have thirty-five relations in Cleator and they include two grandparents, Nana and Granda Close, eleven aunties and uncles, sixteen cousins, great-uncle

Faley and great-auntie Martha, not to mention Mam's cousins and their children, the McAteers. And this is only Cleator, not Cleator Moor, where we have loads more aunties and cousins and Mam's parents, Nana and Papa Heron. So it's safe to say we had the advantage of an extended family, quite literally. Sometimes, I thought, the disadvantages were quite obvious too, because you could get away with nowt!

Bogeys were the thing at the time and they were all very individual contraptions, made from whatever you could scrounge or find abandoned on the tip. My bogey was made from bits of scrap wood left over from when Dad was repairing the lean-to at the back of the house. This lean-to was used to house the dolly tub and mangle which Mam used every Monday in life to do the weekly washing. It also doubled up as a shelter over the outside loo and we kept our bikes and bogeys in it. A few bits of wood were left and a piece of felt, this was ideal because it acted as a cushion on top of the rough pieces of wood and kept the wood dry when we were `on safari' up Jacktrees Road and down Mackinzies Lonnen.

I don't think I've made it quite clear, but a bogey has a platform to sit on and has four wheels. My wheels were given to me by Auntie Winnie, and were from Jimmy's pram, two really huge back wheels and two much smaller ones on the front. The back wheels were the bit you sat on covered by the decking and attached to the axle, which was fixed underneath the frame with fencing staples.

The front wheels were another kettle of fish altogether because they had to be a leg's distance from the seating position so you could steer the bogey with your feet, and to do this the front axle had to be pivoted to give at least forty five degrees movement. This was achieved by putting a bolt through the loose timber cross section which had the front wheels attached to it, in the same way as the back wheels, i.e. fencing staples and the bogey frame. The only way we could drive a hole through the pieces of wood in order to bolt them together was to put the poker into the coal fire and wait until it gets red hot. When it's red hot it will burn a hole through the wood, but it takes loads of goes to burn it right through the two pieces of wood and Mam's watching us like a hawk in case we burn a hole in the hearth rug, not to mention maiming ourselves for life. But she's very patient about this and knows it's the only way to get the hole through. When the holes are finally burnt through it leaves the sides really hard and smooth and doesn't wear through for ages.

LITTLE IRELAND

We had loads of different bogeys - only one at a time mind you, but we used to change the back wheels, for long overland treks we had smaller stronger wheels, and for bogey races we had big prestige pram wheels which you could get a hell of a speed up on. The times I've been hurled off my bogey going round the sharp corners of the paths in Cleator Park is nobody's business.

Of course, the bogeys are one, two or sometimes three manpowered or 'lad-powered', and the speed depends on the length of time the pushers have been pushing. When we go up the Moor we have turns about at pushing and driving.

Early this summer we covered the bogey with a wooden tea chest and we could sit undercover on it and not get wet, but our Barry turned it over and smashed the roof off, so we were back to open air antics. Well, it's far easier to manoeuvre it without the top and sides; actually we used it in the maypole last Friday.

Now Cleator maypoles are not the traditional maypoles people have in other places: no dancing round the maypoles for us. Instead we dress up like you would at a carnival and go door-to-door up and down the backs onto Church Went across Main Street down Kiln Brow, Hilden Road to the Mill, up the Styles, Flosh cottages and back down Main Street to Prospect, collecting pennies and ha'pennies from door-knocking on the way.

I was dressed up as a war hero, in my home-made siren suit made from an old fabric fur coat of my mother's with enough left over for a Davey Crocket hat. I was bloody roasted by the time we got back two hours or more later. Stephen was a cowboy, Margaret was a fairy in her first Holy Communion dress and a crown made from a wedding cake decoration, Mary Stones was Helen of Troy, and Tony Stones had cobbled up a horse mask made of *papier maché,* and mounted it on our bogey, and I think he was a Trojan warrior pulling the Trojan horse. Lucy Kelly had a pink crepe paper, frilly frock and a stick, she was Little Bo Peep. Most of the girls were decked in crepe paper at this mini pageant and that was where the skill came in. Their mothers or older sisters must have spent hours designing and making these elaborate paper costumes.

There was never anything official about them, no judging or competitions of any sort, just a display of sewing skills. Probably originating from the women who worked at the Mill making soldiers' uniforms. Just their little showpieces to the world.

We'd get up on a Saturday morning and the word was out: Prospect is having a maypole today, do you want to join in? And we usually got made up in Anne Howland's back yard or one of the older girl's yard. A few older girls and mams attached the paper outfits to our ordinary clothes. It was great excitement and the money collected was usually divided at the end of the maypole. Maybe the older women took some of the money out for expenses, for the coloured crepe paper and tissue paper, I don't know. We all had a treat from it.

The idea must have had its origins in the days of the proper maypole. I do remember there being proper maypoles at local carnivals, and maybe there would be a pageant after the maypole. So this idea of a village pageant without the maypole must have been a follow on from that. It was great fun. It brought out a wonderful feeling of camaraderie and taught children the natural pecking order of an ordered society. It gave us a chance to be introduced to everybody in the village and to interact with not just our peers, but the older members of the community, and to listen to the comments of the elderly people for whom we had the greatest respect.

Our parents taught us to have the highest respect for the old people, never to be cheeky or answer them back, or even our wit with them, always to be courteous and give our seat up on the bus, or in the doctors surgery. Old people rule, OK.

This always had its up-side because older people can give compliments; they've lost all their inhibitions at this time in their lives, and know how to make a young lad feel worthwhile. I suppose the 'old git' syndrome existed, but it was not pointed out to us and so wasn't such a big issue.

'Treat old people as you would have other people treat your Nana,' Mam used to say.

And we did.

16
RED HILL QUARRY

Needless to say that after the nearly drowning incident with Margaret, the Lonny Beck was out of bounds. But we were so well served with other exciting places to play around about Cleator village that it didn`t really matter.

We had the Red Hill, a perfectly formed mound of quarry waste in the shape of Ayres Rock, and next to it was a huge chimney with a round doorway into it. It was possible to run in and look up at the sky and run back out again. Why? Then there was the sewerage carousel. We used to jump on to it when it was moving and have a ride.

My mate Peter McDowell, couldn't run very fast and so we didn't get into very much trouble because he'd always get caught running away. This saved us both from a misspent youth.

On one of our visits to the sewerage, Peter opened one of the manhole covers and somehow fell in. He was up to his waist in shit as I told my mother later, and got a clout on the back of the head for saying it. I had to pull him out and the smell was diabolical. He was crying and said his mother, Bridey Morgan (everybody gets their maiden name at Cleator), would kill him.

I think she nearly did.

17
THE BLACK SHIP

On route to the Black Ship we would follow the Lonny Beck up stream, real name 'The Keekle Beck'. This part of the river known as the Black Ship, had been re-routed temporarily in 1890 in order to line the bottom and sides of the river bed with concrete and make a wall up the centre to control the water and stop it flooding into the nearby iron-ore pits. It was then re-routed back into its newly formed troughs and remains there to this day.

The name Black Ship was given to this stretch of the beck by the shipbuilders from Whitehaven who made the wooden shutters which were used to cast the concrete. The shutters were covered in tar and resembled the black hull of a ship.

This was an exciting 'Dan Dare' sort of landscape for all over-imaginative little boys. The landscape leading up to the Black ship was more blowsy than immediately round the village, less disturbed by people walking along the edge of the beck.

We could get great peashooters from the rhubarb-like plants near the beck edge, the smallest of which you could hollow out and spit hawthorn berries at any unsuspecting old lady you might pass.

We didn't do this of course, Peter and me. Actually Peter wasn't allowed to go to the Black Ship, his mother knew instinctively that he would never get back. These riverside plants, some of which were like huge umbrellas inside out, were of special interest to me. I was convinced we'd strayed into a tropical rain forest and pigmies would jump out at us at any moment.

The landscape immediately around the Black Ship was totally derelict with small grey slag banks and flat areas with hardly any grass growing, just the odd patch of knapweed and buttercups and ragged robins here and there struggling to survive, God knows how!

This white slag was very light; some of it would even float when you threw it into the water. There were several ponds, not very deep, but they were black and cold looking. The good thing was they had newts and huge frogs. The newts we could catch and take home in a jar, they looked like little prehistoric monsters having legs and being able to survive on both land and underwater.

LITTLE IRELAND

On this particular occasion we could see the remains of some large frogs, they had been blown up. Stephen, Edward Fitzpatrick and myself were shocked by the sight of these creatures with their light green bellies split open. We knew what had happened to them ..'The Moor Row Gang'.

The Moor Row Gang was a constant threat to us, consisting of the big lads from Moor Row who were notoriously vicious and cruel and we were told if you see them when you're out, run like hell. They were a sort of cavalier gang who roamed the countryside around Moor Row and cut the heads off chickens and blew up frogs and battered unsuspecting lads from Cleator, or so they said.

In all my years and expeditions to the Black Ship I never once encountered them, but lived in constant dread of running into them. Anyhow this must have been their cruel work.

Raymond Clark and Trevor Palmer told us how to blow up a frog. You caught the frog, pushed a peashooter into its mouth and down its throat and blew hard down the shooter. The frog's belly goes up like a balloon and if you keep blowing it explodes and splatters guts everywhere. We were totally sickened.

Everything around us looked suddenly alien. We were aware these predators from Moor Row had stood on this very spot. We had to get away as soon as possible from here.

Right at the end of the Black Ship was the dog tunnel, some six feet high by three feet wide hacked into solid rock about twenty yards long, pitch black except for the dot of light at the end. Drips of water caught you unaware and gave you a fright as you slowly inched your way through. Built as a shortcut from the iron ore pits to Moor Row for the weary miners coming on and off their shifts. It looks a poor example of an apprentice piece.

Now tales of smugglers' caves and bandits were rife around here. I once found a full packet of Capstan and a Swiss army knife in a small crack in the wall, so how much more evidence do you need? The only problem was the Moor Row Gang was a constant threat to us, and you would be certain to run into them at the other end of the dog tunnel.

We had originally set out to find the raft that Joe Farren said he found hidden in the bulrushes, and to collect some rosehips. The Council school bought rosehips and paid four pence (four old pence) a pound for them. They sent them away for rosehip syrup and every

LITTLE IRELAND

September when we went back to school the rosehip season was launched and you could make loads of money.

The area between Cleator cricket field and Moor Row along the Lonny Beck was chocker with dog-rose bushes, so by the mid-September it was thick with rosehips. You got ripped to bits with the thorns, but the hunter-gatherer instinct came into play and we could collect pounds of the orange beauties in an afternoon session.

There was a competition for the person who collected the most rosehips and the winner had the dubious honour of being taken on a guided tour of the rosehip factory in Pontefract and presented with a gold rosehip badge. What an incentive!

We had regular moneymaking seasons in those days. In July there was the 'bleeberry' season. They grew up on the fells on the side of Dent just above the Black Wood. They were a real pig to collect, because they stuck like shit to a blanket, as we used to say. The comb was useful, you could hold your tin on its side against the very low bushes and with a swinging motion with your comb, swipe the top of the bush and comb the little purple perishers into your tin. When you got home your hands, lips and teeth would be dyed dark purple. We took them to Bessie Rooney's, the bakers on Main Street, Cleator, and she'd give us a shilling a pound. A much better price than the rosehips, but ten times harder to collect. She made lovely 'bleeberry pie'.

We always kept a pound or so for Mam to make our own 'bleeberry cake'. Most people considered 'bleeberry cake' a real delicacy. I'm not surprised considering how difficult it was to pick the wretched things.

Then there was the 'blackites' as we called them (blackberries). Just after the 'bleeberries' and before the rosehips, about mid to late August. Again a good seller to the local baker at Cleator and Cleator Moor, or just a bagful for Mam's 'blackites' crumble. I'm beginning to sound like Delia Smith. And lastly, thank God, you're thinking, tatie picking week. Half term, October. Ike Poole, Harry Hodgson and Andrew Watson would put the word out they were looking for fit lads and lasses for tatie picking. You got fifteen shillings for a full week, a King's ransom and the most backbreaking and thoroughly enjoyable week on the annual working calendar - except maybe for hay timing. That would be in July and we didn't do that until we were a lot older, much heavier work of course, lifting heavy bales of hay, but the weather was always nice for that. We'd go to Ike Poole's fields with Dad and ride on the hay trucks pulled by the old cart-horse, watch it take our photo as Dad said, when it lifted its tail to break wind and do the 'big job' as it trotted up the cobbles to Blackhow Farm.

18
THE LUCKY ROAD

The Lucky Road was a favourite walk for our family on a Sunday morning.

Mam would start making Sunday dinner after we arrived back from nine o'clock Mass. Dad's job was to entertain us for a couple of hours, so off we'd go. Barry, Stephen, Margaret and myself. Often Shaun Devoy my cousin tagged along because there was a cash incentive to our morning walks.

We'd set off with the intention of finding money on this walk, and we always did. It was a great source of encouragement when we were falling behind and Dad would say 'Look under that stone, Sean, or maybe behind that wall.' We rarely, if ever, found money on the early part of the walk, but we were never disappointed.

Down the Lonny over the bridge and along the Lonny again to the cricket field. Now the Lonny or Lonning between the Lonny Bridge and the cricket field had very high hedges either side and a multitude of wild flowers. There were soldiers buttons, scabby lips and the pissy beds. We weren't allowed to pick some of these for obvious reasons.

There were bluebells, cornflowers, forget-me-nots, violets, speedwell and harebells, and Dad showed us how to hold a sharp piece of grass between both thumbs and blow down it to make a loud whistling noise, which would burst your eardrums. Dad reckoned every plant we found in the hedge meant the hedge was a hundred years old. So it must have been hundreds and hundreds of years old.

We'd pass the cricket field gate and stile and pass the vicarage, which was in an elevated position overlooking the cricket field. It had a lovely flat field in front of it called the Gleebfield, and they used to hold garden parties every summer. There would be hoop-la, and bat-the-rat, cake stalls, and pound stalls, home-made scones and tea for sale, and a tug-of-war, what a treat.

This field also had very good mushrooms in it, and another curiosity of the field was the cow farts, that's what Dad called them. They were little mustard coloured fungi growing in the grass, about the size of a gob-stopper, and when you kicked them, accidentally or otherwise, they exploded and gave off a puff of thick brown smoke

LITTLE IRELAND

with a musty smell. We loved them.

The walk continued alongside the high wall surrounding the vicarage garden and looking back you could see the cricket field below, the Lonny Beck and 'Cleator Daddy's' garden, which by early summer would be full of wallflowers and Sweet Williams. You could actually smell them as you walked past, even though nothing was visible through the privet hedge. Above the garden, St Leonard's church and Cleator village, then Dent, acting as a huge backdrop, its gentle slopes dotted with plantations of fir trees, and drifting off to Kinniside Kop the Ennerdale Valley, and Knock Murton.

Dent Mountain stands 1,029 feet above sea level and is technically the first mountain of the Western Lake District. Cleator village nestles in its foothills and is a wonderful base camp for the adventurous fell walker.

Moving on the Lucky Road had yet to yield any reward, apart from the sights and sounds and smells, not fully appreciated by the young walkers. About a quarter of a mile on, under the railway bridge, there's a disused railway line, with part of the bridge still standing over the Woodend to Moor Row road, and just before you reach the road junction set in the side of the railway embankment was the Quaker's grave. A slab of sandstone inscribed with the words:

Actual inscription on grave stone.
Here Doath the body of John Garner lays,
Who was faithful to the Lord in all his days
Who did this burying place freely bestow
And dispensed the Gospel without charge you know
Unto the people over which he was ordained
A pastor (sic) unto them he did still remain
Buryed ye 2 Day of December 1706
Aged 75 years

The legend of the Quaker's grave was clouded in mystery. The truth may never be known, but the version we were familiar with was this: a family of Quakers living a simple life for generations in the hamlet of Gutterby nearby, had a Quakers' Meeting House on some land bought by the railway company to build the new railway line serving the numerous iron ore mines.

The Meeting House was smack bang in the middle of where the new line was to go. In spite of objections by the Quakers, the railway company decided it would be too costly to re-route the line and so

LITTLE IRELAND

the Meeting House would have to be demolished. This ancient building was considered sacrosanct to the Quakers, and a legal battle lasting twelve months was launched. But the railway company won in the end and when they came to demolish the building John Garner the Pastor, said they would have to pull the building down round him before he would leave.

The delay this hiccup caused was costing the railway company hundreds of pounds and John Garner who had taken up residency in the Meeting House was offered a bribe to try to resolve the problem. He refused the bribe and subsequent bribes and so the decision was taken to demolish the building with John Garner in it. The building was partly demolished and during the night the roof fell in and killed the Quaker before he could be rescued. The railway company were devastated by the accident and had tried everything to avoid this mishap, bringing with it very bad publicity.

So, after his death, they erected the sandstone plaque in his honour on the railway embankment at the very spot where the meeting house had once stood. Dad used to tell us this story every time we passed the sandstone slab, with its old English lettering becoming badly weathered, and not very clear. We all felt this place was a holy place and spoke in low voices out of respect.

Passing the row of houses known as the hamlet of Gutterby, we'd continue on to the railway crossing at Woodend. The railway station where you could get a train to Whitehaven or Workington or Cleator Moor or Egremont or anywhere. We used to go on the Sunday school trip to Seascale from here once a year with St Leonard's Church Trip.

My earliest memories of a railway trip was with Dad, we went to see Workington Reds play Carlisle United at Workington via Moor Row and the Keekle Viaduct through to Moresby Parks, Harrington and then on to Workington. Steam train with single carriage, of course.

We were just approaching the luckiest part of the Lucky Road, between Woodend and Cleator village, about, half-a-mile stretch of open road, with broken pavements, ideal for three - and sixpenny pieces to lodge in, having fallen from unsuspecting travellers to and from the railway, we thought. Sure enough first a 3d piece would be found then two sixpenny pieces, loads of pennies and halfpennies and Stephen once found a half-a-crown. The excitement and thrill of finding these coins was incredible. It's hard to explain just how much fun it was and the expression on the faces of the finders said it all.

LITTLE IRELAND

We didn't need Nintendos and Game Boys and computers, we had the Lucky Road, and the fresh air and vivid imaginations, and a Dad who fired our imaginations with legends of Quakers' graves - and who could be bothered to walk to Woodend station early on Sunday morning before we got up for Mass and drop coins on the pavement on his way back, so that we could find them and think it was truly a 'Lucky Road'.

19
CRAB FAIR

Egremont Crab Fair, an ancient country fair first started over 600 years ago and continued ever since, going from strength to strength. It begins at 12 noon with the traditional crab apple distribution. This consists of a convoy of horse drawn carts loaded up with crab apples and, as far as I can remember, men throw the apples into the crowds. Its origins must go back to the benevolent landowners making some sort of gesture to the peasants. Any how it's great fun.

The carts, or lorries of more modern times, move slowly down the full length of Main Street to the War Memorial. The apple throwers on the lorries throw apples into the crowd on their way. If you're not careful you could get crushed to death in the stampede for the crabs, coxes and Egremont russets, which I always find very sour and dry.

It's quite a spectacle and everybody loves it. Then there's the greasy pole, a long rugby goal post type of pole; about twenty feet long stood on end and covered in axle grease. The object of the game is to climb to the top of the pole with a Hessian sack between your legs to protect your pants from the grease, and collect the leg of lamb or half a suckling pig, which is impaled on the very top of the pole. The first lad to do this gets to keep the lofty prize.

The day is punctuated with various sports events and dog shows and the usual hound trail, cycle races and fell races etc, but the highlight of the whole fair is the 'gurning'. Egremont Crab Fair is the only venue in the world of this bizarre competition, or at least it was when I was a lad.

You need a horse yoke through which to place your head, and then you set a funny face. It helps if you have false teeth because you can make a very funny face it you remove your dentures, and pull your top lip up and over your head and force your bottom lip into your left ear. I've seen it done.

You can see by my descriptions that this is not the cultural event of the year. The Eisteddfod or Edinburgh Tattoo it is not! But it is our own brand of tongue-in-cheek entertainment and could be described as 'alternative' humour; very fashionable today, actually. When you think about it, it's no worse than 'Vic Reeves' Big Night Out', with his 'Fantasy Island' and the 'Dove from above'.

Last year the gurning was televised live on 'The Big Breakfast'. Whatever next? I found myself asking.

My most memorable Crab Fair took place when I was about nine years old. Dad always took us. We caught the 11.30 bus from Cleator, if the weather looked dodgy, but if it was a fine morning we walked the two miles and speculated all the way who would be first up the greasy pole. We walked this particular year and Dad was not his usual jolly self for some reason. It transpired he had toothache and felt the vibration of every step on his back molars. When we arrived at Egremont Main Street, Dad sat Barry, Stephen and myself on the low sandstone wall by the Police Station and told us not to move until he got back. He said he was going to Frank Tolsen's the dentist, to see if he could prescribe something for his toothache. He must have been away for an hour and a half; the crab apples had long since been thrown and people were beginning to wonder what three lone, small boys were doing lurking about for such a long time.

When Dad finally arrived he had a bloody handkerchief up to his mouth and he looked as if he'd been in a fight. Eventually when he was able to speak, he explained that he'd gone into the dentist's and as luck would have it, George Tolsen had had a cancellation and was able to fit Dad in there and then.

After a quick look in his mouth Mr Tolsen had announced he would advise having the lot out to save Dad any further trouble, and he assured Dad false teeth are much easier to look after than your own. Dad was in such pain he would have let him pull his fingernails out if he thought it would ease the pain, so he gave his consent.

He couldn't talk very well as you can imagine. His whole mouth had been numbed with cocaine. He said he had to be sick and disappeared behind the stone wall. When he reappeared he'd been sick all down his jumper and it was covered in blood and sick. He said, 'Listen lads, I'm going for a pint. I feel bloody awful, so have a walk down to the War Memorial and watch the lads climbing the greasy pole for a while; I'm going into the *Bluebell.*

We watched Raymond Clark and Joe Rooney from Cleator attempt the pole, but they didn't quite reach the top despite our cheering and willing them on. Eventually Dad came looking for us. He looked a bit better, if you can look better when somebody has just ripped your teeth from your head only an hour or so earlier. He was at least better able to talk, but he sounded really funny. I didn't like the look of him.

His handsome face was all distorted and puffed up. What the hell will Mam say? She wouldn't be expecting this, I know!

To say she was 'gobsmacked' when we all arrived back home and she realised what Dad had done was the understatement of the century. She was speechless and visibly shocked.

She said, 'For God's sake Jay, could he not have saved the front ones, you only had toothache in one of your back teeth didn't you?'

Dad replied, 'Aye well the rest weren't that good lass and old Tolsen said they'd give me trouble sooner or later, so I thought I'd better get the lot out.'

He was only 37 years old at the time and I remember him having really nice big front teeth and they seemed very white. In those days if you could afford to get your teeth out before they gave you any trouble, you never had them filled. Pull the lot out and get a new tile grate in while you're at it, that's what they used to say.

20
RECURRING DREAMS

I've just had a horrible dream. I've had this dream before and it frightens me. It's not exactly the same every time, but bits of it keep coming back. The dream always includes Papa Heron and I'm sure something terrible is going to happen to him. I remember every detail of it when I waken.

Papa's car couldn't get through into Prospect backs because an old single-decker bus was blocking the entrance. There was Papa and Nana and Stephen and me in Papa's car and it was getting dark. Nana Heron gave Stephen and me a chloradine sweet, she called them chloradines, but they had the name 'Victory V' on the packet, and they were so strong they nearly burned your throat. This sweet was nearly making my nose pop and I couldn't talk, I thought I was going to choke but I couldn't shout out. The burning in my stomach and throat spread into my lungs, and I thought my lungs would collapse.

I spat it out and Nana picked it off the car floor and put it in her mouth and told me off for spitting it out. For some reason she wasn't in the dream any more, just Papa, Stephen and me.

Papa's old black Ford felt comfortable with its dark blue leather seats and its big driving wheel. It was warm and safe. For some reason Papa didn't have his cap on. He always wore his cap, except in the house and at church. He wasn't bald, he had plenty of hair on the sides and his hair went into a sort of kiss curl on his forehead. I was thinking how strong he was and how much I loved him. He was great. He used to sing a song to us when he took us for a walk.

His favourite trick was to hold our hands and let us walk across the top of the handrail over the Iron Bridge on Kiln Brow, and every now and again he would pretend to push us over. We would scream and he would laugh. The song he used to sing was:

Over the brook to Grandmama, over the brook little boy
The flowers are sweet beneath my feet we sing as we go for joy
Ta ra ra ra ra Ta ra ra ra ra
We sing as we go for joy

Papa was seventy last Friday and he took all the grandkids, lads that is, to the top of Dent and we took pasche eggs with us to roll. Mam had spent all morning boiling the eggs and dyeing them this dark brown colour with onion skins. Dad says he's a fit old bugger is 'old Stiven'.

'Papa doesn't kiss,' he always said that. He hugs us and he'd hold our hands, but he never kisses.

Mam told me that he believed that old people carried germs and shouldn't breathe them on children. But Nana kisses us and everybody else does. I wished Papa did.

Papa has this imaginary 'bogey' man who he calls 'Shino', and if he doesn't want us to do something or go somewhere he tells us 'Shino' is watching us, and 'Don't go in there mind, 'Shino's' in there,' and we run to him and climb up on his back screaming with terror. But we know it's just a game, 'cos there's no such thing as a bogey man.

But I think I've seen 'Shino'. He's called old Isaac and he does the building repairs on Prospect, I think he works for Carty Wilson or one of the landlords. I've seen him coming out of our hut in the back yard, where Papa says 'Shino' lives. He must be the real 'Shino'. He looks evil. I hope I never run into him on a dark night. Or maybe Shino's the only tramp who comes round the backs playing an accordion. People feel sorry for him and give him coppers. He has a look of Isaac about him. They might even be the same person.

Back to the dream ... The single-decker bus was crowded and Papa got out of the car and asked a very, very thin woman in a black uniform how long would they be parked, because he needed to get past. She made some very bad tempered reply and Papa got back into the car looking a bit upset and said, 'I'll go down Church Went and on to the backs. Do you lads want to get out here?'

So Stephen and me got out and looked in amazement at the strange group of passengers disembarking from the bus. They were all deformed children. Some were crawling along on their bellies, one with a huge head and just a few tufts of hair, a set of Siamese twins joined together in the middle, sharing three legs and two heads but just one body. Loads of skinny ill-looking children, all very well dressed and clean. We followed the tide of deformed children and helpers down to the beck, where along the beck edge were big reptile-like creatures, like large lizards only much fatter, about a chubby child's size. They talked to each other and jumped up at me like a dog trying to steal food from my mouth.

There were two animals, half-dog and half-human. Why are they going down to the beck in the dark? TO BE DROWNED. And where's Papa? Something's happened to Papa.

I'm awake sitting up in bed and in a lather of sweat. Mam comes running in and she says I haven't to eat cheese last thing at night any more.

My Nice Dream

Now this dream I have quite often and I love it. I know I'm going into this dream because I'm aware that I'm actually dreaming. I'm sort of awake and telling myself, well maybe I'll believe it or may be I won't, but I can't resist dreaming it.

I'm standing either in the house or on the backs, or lying in bed, suddenly I'm aware that I'm standing about three or four inches off the ground. No-one else seems to notice, so I'm just enjoying this relaxing feeling. I can float around forever like this, taking hardly any effort to move from side to side, or back and forwards, but I can't resist the call of the wild, so I know by now, I've done it so often, how to get higher off the ground. I lift my arms up, then my knees and make a downward movement with my legs pushing myself upwards. It doesn't feel like flying, I'm not in a horizontal position like a bird, I'm bolt upright.

When I'm in the house I reach the ceiling in seconds, I've got to keep the pressure on my hands to maintain height, but its no real effort, I can relax my hands slightly and reduce my height or bear down with them and squeeze myself tight into the ceiling and see the cobwebs round one corner of the living room. If I'm not careful I'll get burned by the light bulb, I've been burned before like this. I bet Mam hasn't seen these cobwebs.

But outside it's better, I can get above the houses and feel the wind, but then I haven't got the bottle to fly really high, I come back slowly to earth and reflect on how much I enjoyed this gift I have and look forward to my next dream when I take to the sky. Then I wake up with a feeling of excitement in my heart.

I don't tell anybody about my nice dream because I have this feeling that if I talk about it I won't be able to get the dream back, and

I'm hoping to build on this dream. I'm quite convinced that if I can get this feeling in my hands that starts me off on my out-of-body experience in my dream, when I'm awake I'll definitely be able to float in real life. It's just a matter of concentration in my next nice dream and transferring this sensation into reality. It's got to be possible, and the possibilities are endless.

21
WORKINGTON INFIRMARY

Just before my eighth birthday, I ended up in hospital. I can't remember anything about being in an ambulance or the journey to Workington, at the dead of night - last night as it happens - or anything much at all about last night, except I remember a lot of shouting.

I'm not sure who was doing the shouting or what was being said. I think it could have been me.

Workington Infirmary looked just as I would imagine a workhouse to look. Green tiles halfway up the walls, with a black border tile then lavatory-green paint above that. It's enough to make you badly if you're not badly already, but that's just it, I'm not badly, or at least I don't feel badly. If I'd been badly, I wouldn't have taken so much notice of my surroundings, being too badly to notice. Actually, I felt great, albeit a bit confused. I needed some questions answered, and I want out of here asap.

I was in a four-bed ward with just me in it. I was sitting up in bed like 'Piffey on a rock bun.' The only sound I could hear was that of a train slowing down, going past the window. I could see through the ward door and through the window of the next room. I felt as if I'd been abandoned.

Why isn't Mam here?

Why am I here at all?

Am I in this hospital (workhouse) on my own, or is there someone else here as well?

Because I was in bed I felt I should stay put. Maybe I can't walk! I'd got a pair of pyjamas on, not my own, and not a very good fit either. It was just like that film where the man is suffering from amnesia and can't remember anything about his past life - except I could remember everything apart from the last few hours, or maybe I'd been in a coma for weeks. I'd soon convinced myself that that was not the case as the butterfly transfer I had put on my forearm was still intact, so I hadn't lost that much time.

These observations and thoughts were taking place in just a few seconds, not even minutes, but they seemed to be taking forever. Eventually a nice young nurse came to my bed and said, 'You're awake I see. You had us a bit worried for a while. How do you feel now?'

I replied, 'I'm alright. Where am I? And where's my Mam?'

The young nurse went on to explain that I'd arrived during the night by ambulance, after having some sort of fit; at least that's what the doctor thought last night. My Mam and granddad had gone back to Cleator and would be back to see me some time later today, 'After the doctor had done some tests and examined me again'.

I wanted to know where everyone was, why the other beds were empty, whose pyjamas I was wearing, could I get out of bed and could I have something to eat? To which the nurse replied, 'You're in the Emergency Admissions Ward under special surveillance until we can find out what is wrong with you. That's why there's no-one else in the other beds. You were the only admission last night, but you'll be put into the main children's ward as soon as Dr Robinson sees you in about half an hour. Mind, I don't think, looking at you, you'll be here for very long.'

I started to cry. A wave of sadness came over me and transported me into a flood of tears.

Seeing me cry, the nurse tried to reassure me, 'Here now don't worry, you're going to be alright.'

I didn't want her to see me cry. I didn't even know why I was crying. I bit back the tears and asked the nurse if I could get out of bed. But she said, 'I don't think you should do that until the doctor has seen you. Be a good lad and settle back and I'll bring you a glass of milk, and as soon as the doctor comes we'll get you some Cornflakes and toast.'

After the doctor and three or four young students had poked and prodded me, pushed sticks down my throat and fingers up my bum, I was pronounced 100% fit.

A slight scratch was detected on my left forearm. I was asked how I got the scratch, to which I replied, `Our cat, Sooty, scratched me yesterday, Doctor.'

An expression of sudden inspiration appeared on Dr Robinson's face and he declared, 'You've had Cat Scratch Fever. A bad case of Cat Scratch Fever caused by the infection from the cat scratch, which caused you to have a severely high temperature and in turn, caused the fit.' He continued, 'Let his parents know my diagnosis, Nurse, when they come, and they can take him home anytime after midday. Tell them to give him plenty of fluids and he can have some breakfast'.

The doctor and students routinely moved away from my bed and continued to discuss the Cat Scratch Fever theory until they disappeared from view and ear-shot. I don't really remember where I got the scratch. It could have been from Sooty or from a bramble, or a belt buckle, or anything, but I didn't care to complicate matters by telling Dr Robinson this and besides, I was going home and that's all that mattered.

The young nurse's name was Connelly and, as it happened, she came from Cleator Moor and knew my family. She was nice and after she gave me my breakfast she let me help her roll bandages. For some reason, I was never transferred to the main ward, probably because I wasn't being detained long enough. I felt as if I'd had some unique and individual experience. A bit unreal, as if I'd had the entire hospital to myself.

When Mam, Papa and Nanna Heron arrived in Papa's car to take me home, armed with a Dinky toy bus (one like Papa's), they were all equally surprised and relieved with the diagnosis. Dad's reaction was a bit different. When we arrived home and Mam told him what the doctor had said, his comment was, 'Cat Scratch Fever, my arse!'

22
THE ATTIC STAIRS

The attic stairs at 30 Prospect Row had a cat winder, that is a turn at the bottom of 45 degrees. It had a strip of carpet up the middle, and was painted either side in magnolia. The carpet was made up of a symmetrical pattern and it was a work of art the way it had been fitted to the shape of the staircase.

We slept in the attic, Stephen, Barry and myself. The balustrade went round at a right angle and from the third step down I could see the whole of the floor area from ground level. At the far end was a window which had a semicircular head and went right down to the ground - and a sliding sash. From this angle the bright yellow lino floor covering would shine 'like a new pin'.

We had a double bed for myself and Stephen and a single bed for Barry, or whichever combination we worked out nightly. Close to the top of the stairs Mam had screened part of the room with a ceiling-to-floor yellow-flowered curtain. This formed a square storage area. Behind the curtain was an 'Aladdin's Cave' of junk, an old black, men's bicycle; it weighed a ton. There was a Singer hand-sewing machine, boxes of books, sledges and tents, lots of old toys and an old mahogany chest of drawers, very tidy piles of clothes in boxes; last winter's clothes put away for next year to be recycled, a box with odd rolls of wallpaper and the one toy I held onto for years. I would not let Mam throw away my Mobo crazy car - possibly the best Christmas present I was ever given. It was a tin car painted red and orange with a cord attached to drag it along with. The unique feature of my Mobo crazy car was the way it shot from side to side making siren noises. I've never seen anything like it since.

It was a hot summer morning and my mind was focused on the possible adventures of the day. The air was extremely humid in the attic room in summer and freezing cold in winter, no proper insulation and very little ventilation.

Mam and Dad were having a lie-in and I had been sent back to bed for another hour's sleep. I had that feeling of frustration you get when you don't feel tired and everybody else is snoring away, and you want the day to start. I was beginning to get bored with this forced imprisonment because the 'crack' on the backs the night before had

LITTLE IRELAND

been about the raft on the Lonny Beck, and everybody was going rafting as soon as we had had breakfast.

Shaun Devoy was coming down for us and we were going to hunt for oil drums down at the Forge. We needed extra buoyancy you see. In the meantime, I'm stuck here looking out onto the cock ring from the attic window and aching to make a start. Barry wasn't going with us because he was going to Blackpool for a week with Tommy and Molly Hannah. They used to live next door at one time and had no children of their own, so they sort of adopted Barry. They bought him birthday presents and Christmas presents and gave him pocket money, took him on holidays and generally spoiled him. Mam and Dad didn't seem to mind them indulging Barry and totally ignoring the rest of us. In retrospect it was a very strange arrangement. I suppose they were a childless couple and Barry was one of four children and could be spared to be given a good time.

Molly was quite fat and wore winged diamante-type glasses and giggled a lot; rather like a silly schoolgirl. She had a friend who lived next door to her on Church Went, Sissy Morgan, and they did everything in tandem. They cleaned the windows together, did the washing together, changed their curtains on the same day, did their shopping together, decorated their living rooms together. Mam said they were 'joined at the hip'.

Molly and Tommy were the butt of Vince McCarty's current joke. Mam and Dad had been for a drink to Hillen's Pub on Main Street. It must have been a special occasion because they rarely went out together, but Mam had been tickled to bits with Joe's rendition of Molly and Tommy's Silver Wedding celebrations. Molly had baked a fruitcake and iced it and decorated it with silver balls. Unfortunately, she ran out of silver balls and because Bessie Rooney's was closed, she hit on the idea of using small ball bearings, of which Tommy had an endless supply in a jar in the hut. She finished decorating the cake and said to Tommy, 'Don't forget which bit has the ball bearings on it, so we won't give it to anyone.'

She had invited her neighbours in for a sherry and a piece of anniversary cake and she and Tommy went over to Hillens' later for a celebratory booze up. Everything was fine until the following morning when Molly bent over to lay the fire, farted and shot the cat. Well, this was the funniest joke Mam had ever been told and I have to admit I loved it. To think of Molly actually farting, never mind

LITTLE IRELAND

shooting the cat, whose name incidentally was 'Lucky', was hysterical. There's something about fat ladies breaking wind that always makes me laugh.

Molly and Sissy Morgan did work at home (today they would be called 'Out-workers'), employed by the paper-mill down Kilnbrow. It was delivered in large cardboard boxes once a week and picked up the following week. Very handy for two ladies who had a lot of time on their hands. They did the home-work together, of course. They mostly assembled paper parasols in the summer and Christmas decorations in the winter.

Mam decided she'd have a go one Christmas for a bit of extra money, so around the beginning of November these boxes started to arrive. There was a minimum requirement of returned boxes per week and by the day before they were due to be collected, we were all seconded to twisting duties. The decorations were made of flat strips of fluorescent thin tin foil, reds and dark greens, about twelve inches long by about an inch wide. The skill was in the twisting. You had to hold the strips tight with your left hand at one end and twist the strips into a spiral with the other, then press them into a tight round flat shape for boxing. They then had to be boxed in dozens in another container for collection. Apparently they were used mostly for decorating pubs and shops. When you unfurled them and hung them onto a ceiling or bar front, they would swing and sparkled with the least bit of breeze. Nice, eh?

You needed to be working or twisting for at least ten hours a day to make any real money, and the house would be completely taken over by cardboard boxes, as were Molly's and Sissy's. Mam neither had enough time nor enough room for this part-time occupation but she was a trier and not afraid of hard work. Mam didn't do the parasols, she just didn't want the house cluttered up all summer, but Molly and Sissy did.

Where on earth these hundreds of paper pleated parasols ended up, God knows. I'm sure I remember Molly saying they mostly went to China and India. They were very pretty; they had a kaleidoscopic pattern of every colour imaginable and were full adult size. They would make fabulous room decorations today.

I'm still looking out of the attic window. The allotments, or gardens as we called them, were about ten yards away from the front of Prospect Row and the grassed strip between the houses and the garden was the clothes drying area; criss-crossed with washing lines all at different angles. The gardens were a microcosm of village past times. There was hen runs, vegetable plots, dog huts for greyhounds and hound trailing dogs, pigeon gardens. My grandfather, Tom Close, and all his sons, Dad included, were into pigeons in a big way. Their gardens were very tidy with beautiful lawns for the 'buds' to land on and pick corn from. They were very careful not to leave any rubbish or foodstuff lying about for fear of rats, but some of the gardens were a disgrace.

There were also some tin sheeting garages and a sort of 'builder's yard' owned by Carty Wilson. The stark contrast between the hen runs, which had that distinctive sulphur smell, and just mud plains, not a blade of grass in sight, and the well-tended vegetable and flower gardens often next to each other, was amazing. The path linking the gardens was well-trodden soil and had small, smooth hollows in it here and there, which were ideal for playing marbles. Gardeners often filled these in (to our annoyance) with ashes from their coal fires. Nothing lasts, does it?

From our attic window on this warm summer, August morning, I could see Katie McCann hanging her washing out to dry. She lived four doors up from us and her husband John McAteer, was Mam's cousin. They had two daughters, Anne and Rosealine and John loved to have his hair combed. As soon as you'd go into their house he'd get the comb out and say, 'Come on lads, see if you can find any nits.' He would roar with laughter. We had some sophisticated games in those days!

I could see the mishmash of washing lines (some people used to cut the grass to make access easier, others didn't bother) and the shambolic eyesore of the gardens immediately beyond. I could see far beyond to the cricket field and Moor Row and I was immediately transported away from Lenny Farren, who was clipping his Lakeland Terriers for the County Show at Ennerdale, to my world of rafts and Amazonian jungle, and fighting off crocodiles, with Billy Robinson and with a bit of luck, Eileen Flemming.

If I could only persuade someone to waken up and get this show on the road.

By this time I'm really 'cheesed off', so I start making pumping noises and coughing, in order to disturb Stephen and Barry. After all, how can they possibly be asleep when I'm wide-awake, hyped up

LITTLE IRELAND

and ready to go, chafing at the bit, the lot!

The little skylight on the back roof is open to let in a bit of fresh air, but it only really succeeds in letting in sounds from the backs, which can be very frustrating when you can't see where the sound is coming from. Then just like magic, Joe Mathers starts his Saturday morning trumpet practice. Joe lives on Main Street at the bottom end, back to back with us on Prospect Row. Then there's the Kelly's, and Mr and Mrs Mawsley's fish and chip shop either side of the Mathers'. There's Annie Geen's sweet shop, Raymond Bradley's house, Sep Todd's, wee Mary's, Joe Graham's shop, Gina White's.

Gina only had one arm. She lost her right arm in an accident at the Mill. The little fat stump that was left was a never-ending source of fascination to me. How did she bear the pain of having her arm ripped off and live to tell the tale? She used to make hooky mats and could also knit with the knitting needle tucked under the stump. She was really amazing.

Mrs Howland and her daughter Anne occupied the end house, next to the gap between the top end and the bottom end of Main Street, and the entrance to Prospect Row. Their house was like a second home to me, I just drifted in and out. Anne took me out for walks and bought me sweets, and we laughed a lot. She was much older than I was, and was like an older sister really.

Joe Mathers

The Latin-American influence was very much in vogue with the pop music of the time. Joe Mathers played with the Blue Rockets, a very popular band, playing such venues as Egremont Market Hall, the Empress Ballroom in Whitehaven and the Carnegie Theatre in Workington, in fact anywhere they could pull a crowd of jive mad teenagers. Teenagers were invented in the 50s; they only started to get a bad press in the 60s. I think Lonnie Donegan was to blame! 'Cumberland Gap' was far too fast to jive to. It sent normal teenagers into a frenzy and unhinged some of them, encouraging them to invent new dances like the Twist; the beginning of the end.

This particular morning Joe was practising 'Cherry Pink and Apple Blossom White.' His performance was breathtaking. Eddie Calvert eat your heart out!

I ran down the attic stairs to the landing window overlooking the backs and I could see Joe through the window in his back bedroom, with the window down, belting out those notes, holding onto the

Piiiiiiiiiiink and the Apple Blossom White. Fantastic!

It seemed quite incongruous to me looking onto that shabby old back street, with its dull sandstone walls and the tiny little sliding sash windows contrasting with the happy shiny Latin sounds coming from Joe's trumpet. He should have been playing with Edmundo Ross, not the Blue Rockets.

This rude awakening had at least kick-started my day and I ran back upstairs to get dressed. On with my khaki shorts, tee-shirt and black sandshoes. The day was about to begin and I was ready for it.

23
MILES BOWDEN

I was too excited for breakfast, but managed to wolf down an overripe banana and a drink of milk. Dad wanted me to go to Miles Bowden's for a packet of razor blades and Mam said, 'Get your hair cut whilst you're there.'

This wasn't too bad because Miles did a mean crew cut and I liked the 'crack' in Miles'.

Dad said, 'See how many's in and if there's any more than two, bring the razor blades back first.'

Needless to say Miles' was full. By 9.15 on Saturday morning it was standing room only. Every man and boy in Cleator had a haircut at least once every three weeks and sometimes once a fortnight. So Miles' sister served customers on Saturday mornings.

You could buy anything at Miles Bowden's, from a bicycle pump to a ping-pong ball. He had a wonderful sense of humour, it was fascinating listening to the political discussions with the older men, and the way he could worm all the crack out of the young lads like Harry Rooney and Roy Hodgson. Who they'd been out with the night before, 'You want to be careful of lasses like her, she eats young lads like you for breakfast,' sweeping the back of the neck with his soft hairbrush, showing them the view from the back with a hand mirror. 'That alright for you, sir?' What can you say if he'd made a right cow's arse of it? You couldn't offend him.

Miles' little barber shop with its red-and-white striped pole outside was on the other side of Main Street. It must have originally been two houses knocked into one, the two front rooms being occupied by the barber shop on one side of the door and the curiosity shop on the other side.

Both rooms were small and packed to the gills with stuff. The shop part had only about three square feet of floor space to stand in just as you went through the door, but it didn't matter what you wanted, Miles knew where it was.

His sister would shout through, `Miles, have we got any white cotton?'

'Yes lass, near the window in the orange box, underneath the box of candles and the Dr Whites,' whatever they were!

The barber shop itself, the inner sanctum, where every subject under the sun was discussed from the Suez Crisis to Gertie Greenlow's hats. It had two large mirrors on opposite walls which made the room look fifty times bigger than it actually was. These mirrors had stickers placed here and there around the edge, advertisements for Ryzler cigarette papers and Swan Vesta matches. You could see everyone in the shop from a sitting position including the backs of their heads. When Miles finished his gentleman's hair cut, brushed him down and Brylcreemed him, he would say, 'Can I get you anything for the weekend, sir?'

This always puzzled me.

Sometimes the man would say, 'Er, yes', and cough, being rather embarrassed.

Miles would climb on the footstool and reach into a small box on the top shelf and remove a very small packet of 'something'. I never managed to actually see the packet, but he popped it into a brown paper bag and charged him 1/6d. The haircut was only 6d so whatever he was buying in such a small packet must have been quite valuable.

I got the razor blades and took them back to Dad and managed to persuade Mam that I'd be too late for confession if I'd stayed for a haircut. The sooner I go to confession the sooner we can start rafting.

24
THAT TOUCHY THING

Stephen and I went to confession once a fortnight, on Saturday mornings. It was our week this week and we didn't mind, we knew we'd been naughty and had said rude words and told lies (only little ones), and we knew we'd feel better after confessing them. This would make us try harder not to commit them again.

Shaun Devoy was supposed to be taking us, but as soon as we arrived at the church he said, 'You two go in, I'm going down the beck for half an hour, I'll meet you back here at half past ten.' He had long since kicked confession into touch.

Stephen and I were kneeling in the third row, which meant there were at least fifteen people before us, not too bad because there were three priests, and a steady stream of confessees parading in and out of the confessional. Well, stone me, mine was Father McCann!

I hated getting Father McCann because, although my sins were never too serious, I liked the anonymity of the more obscure priest, who didn't know me personally, and I knew Father McCann could recognise my voice. Should I tell him about my encounter with Eileen Flemming, that touchy thing? I didn't understand it myself, maybe next time.

Three Hail Mary's and one Our Father later and I'm back outside the church porch waiting for Stephen, who arrived only seconds later. He'd gone in after me and I said, 'What penance did you get, you weren't long?'

He said, 'It was Father Ainsworth, he only gives you one Our Father unless you tell him you've been swearing, so I didn't let on this week.'

I thought, you and me both.

You could see Shaun Devoy (he always got his full title so as not to confuse him with me, we being cousins) making his way up the footpath from the mill beck. Stephen said, 'Come on, we'll see if he's going to look down the forge for some oil drums'. Good as his word, Shaun led the way back through Cleator, past Old Hall, Auntie Mary and Nana Close' houses, down the hill and we were there.

25
A RAFTING EXPERIENCE

The Old Forge had long since ceased making spades and garden forks and was totally dilapidated. Most of the glass in the old foundry and outbuilding was smashed and heaps of rusting lengths of metal and wire were scattered everywhere. Albert Palmer had said he'd seen lots of empty oil drums, great big ones lying around all over the place. This was a gross exaggeration. We found three, mind you they were huge. One had a hole through it, another one had no lid, but we could bodge them up with tape and keep the holes to the top away from the water.

We all went back over the sewerage field and along the bottom of the back field to the Low Lodge Bridge. The beck was deepest just past Low Lodge house and we had already collected two old doors, four sleepers and a selection of bits of wood.

We discovered to our dismay that the sleepers were too heavy, because although they floated, their sheer weight pushed the oil drums too far under the water and we would be standing in two feet of water.

No good! Back to the drawing board!

By this time quite a large group of lads had gathered to watch the activity. Joe Rooney and Joe Farren said if a gang of us went with them they knew where they could get hold of some pallets, these would be ideal. We could strap the drums to the bottom of the pallets and they would provide a natural platform to stand on. The tension was mounting. Ren Palmer and Nancy Coghlan arrived with two old car seats and Mary Stones brought a load of rope. It took about two hours, or so I suppose, to actually gather everything together.

The three drums were strapped onto the pallets and carefully positioned so as not to let the holes near the water line. The pallets were braced with the odd bits of wood and we kept two bits of wood for punts. I could hardly bear the excitement; we were actually going to float down the beck on this deathtrap.

We turned the raft drum-side down and tied the car seats to the deck. Now who was going to be first on? Fair's fair, Stephen and Shaun Devoy and I had started the whole thing off, so we were elected to crew its maiden voyage. About ten of us lifted it onto the beck and it floated nine or ten inches proud of the water. What an achievement!

Joe Rooney pushed me, 'Go on lad, don't be a shit.'

So I jumped on and hardly made any impression on the water level, next Stephen and then Shaun Devoy. Shaun and I had a punt apiece, we'd already tied a piece of rope to the front end (or was it the back end) and secured it to a tree at the edge of the beck. Now it was well secured. It felt really safe and as long as we didn't make any sudden movements, it floated beautifully.

The beck at this point was very slow moving, and the stretch of water, about thirty or forty yards with no rocks standing up, was the best the Lonny had to offer. Raymond Clark slipped the rope and we set sail, amidst shouts of, 'Me next mind' from Big Joe Rooney, and 'Hurry up you jammy gets' from Brian Fletcher.

It felt wonderful. Shaun Devoy pushed us away from the bank and our clumsy punts enabled us to manoeuvre the craft into the middle of the beck. A terrifying two feet of water at least, was underneath us. Stephen was rigidly sitting on one of the car seats like 'King Dick', making no attempt to move. Raymond Fletcher threw a boulder, which landed inches away from the raft and soaked both Stephen and me. We were then bombarded with boulders for about ten minutes, which we good-humouredly endured until we'd had enough. By this time we were really soaked. We'd had our turn.

I kept thinking, as soon as they all go home, we'll come back and just float up and down. It'll be great.

Everyone was to have a turn. After about two hours all the lads had had a go, so it was the lasses' turn. Mary Stones wasn't for it, she said. 'Let Ren and Nancy have a go first, and then I'll go on with our Tommy.'

Ren Palmer was a big lass, but Nancy Coghlan was huge. The oil drums had taken on a bit of bilge and the raft was definitely not riding as high as it had been at first, but this was no matter. It had had Big Joe Rooney and Albert Palmer and Joe Farren on all at once. So it should take Ren and Nancy's weight, it was decided. You could see the lads going in for the kill.

Big Joe was standing in the water holding the raft steady so that the two lasses could climb aboard. Ren went first amidst screams and giggles and words of encouragement from the bank. The raft tilted but

LITTLE IRELAND

as soon as she sat down it settled down, albeit a bit lopsided. The raft had to be turned round so that Nancy didn't have to climb over Ren. This was done and Nancy threw herself onto the boat and nearly turned the craft over.

Everybody cheered while Big Joe settled the big lass into a sitting position next to Ren on the car seats. Joe must have known the drums were taking in water because the raft was only a couple of inches above water level, but he shoved the raft for a minute or so until Ren realised they didn't have a punt and the raft was gathering speed. At the end of the pool the beck tumbled over rocks before forming another pool rather smaller than the one we were using. It was obvious by now that the raft was out of control, and panic was setting in.

Ren hurled abuse at Joe Rooney and Nancy threatened him with a good pummelling if he didn't get in and stop them, but they were hurtling towards the rapids. Mary Stones threw the punt for Ren to catch, but caught her on the back of the head and knocked her forward. The rest of the scene seemed to be happening in slow motion. Nancy tried to reach the punt and slewed round on the car seat, the seat came free from the raft bottom and Nancy fell back in the seat and rolled into the water. Ren tried to stop her going overboard and hurled herself headfirst after her. The bank was in an uproar.

Big Joe, Raymond Clark, the three Palmer's lads and Joe Farren were in like a shot. Mary Stones was hysterical. I didn't know whether to laugh or cry. Shaun Devoy nearly peed himself laughing and the raft broke up on the rocks with one of the oil drums zooming along on its own at a rate of knots towards the cricket field.

The lasses were alright, but left sitting in about eighteen inches of dirty water; the only thing that was injured was their pride. But take what Big Joe got from Nancy and Ren, all the stinky pigs they could turn their tongues to.

No-one had any spare clothes, so Mary Stones ran home and brought a huge frock she'd borrowed from Eunice Horicks for Nancy, and something for Ren from her own house. They made their way over to the bulrushes to get dried off and my first sexual experience was about to happen.

Joe Farren came running over to the lads and asked, 'Who wants to see big Nancy in the pelt? She's over the other side of the beck getting dried off'.

Well, what can you do? If I hadn't gone I'd have been called a pansy, so I succumbed to 'peer pressure'. That's my story and I'm sticking to it!

I'd never seen a female in the pelt before, not even my sister, so what I was about to see nearly put me off women for life. There she was in all her glory blissfully unaware of the gang of lads peeping through the tall grass and bulrushes. A small gap in the undergrowth revealed Nancy drying herself down with an old Hessian sack.

The image will stay with me forever. Those huge breasts and milky white folds of fat, no obvious sign of a waist, tons of cellulite and a wisp of pubic hair. I was nearly sick.

Well, so much for the raft. It doesn't pay you to get your hopes up too much. It should have lasted at least for a full weekend, if not two. All that work and just ten minutes pleasure down the Swannie or in this case, down the Lonny.

26
ECCENTRICS

Cleator was not without its eccentrics and characters.

There was Wee Gertie Greenlaw who lived in the little lodge house attached to Ehenhall Mansion. The lodge house was like a doll's house and suited Gertie down to the ground. It could have been purpose-built for her. She would be no more than 4ft 6ins tall I suspect, 'Next thing til' a dwarf' as my Dad described her - long before the days of political correctness. She would be described today as 'vertically challenged'. It doesn't have the same ring to it somehow, does it?

Gertie had a way with hats; her outfits were extraordinary. I remember coming out of Joe Graham's shop one morning and walking straight into her. If it hadn't been for that hat I would have knocked her flying and she'd have measured her length on the pad. I apologised for giving her a fright, and she was concerned that I was alright. I was alright, but rather taken aback because this was the first time I had been really close to Gertie. I realised that she was quite an old woman, not the young girlish figure I had always perceived her to be.

Her hats could easily have been 3ft in diameter and often had a full veil covering her face. That day she had a bright pink broad-rimmed hat with veil. The veil was white with dark pink polka dots, and her coat was the same dark pink as the polka dots on her veil. To complete the outfit a pair of bright red shoes with huge chunky heels. She looked like a combination of Barbara Cartland, Mrs Shilling and a Toby jug all rolled into one. Her sense of colour co-ordination and mix 'n' match was immaculate.

There was a rather rude joke going around at the time about Gertie. Apparently she had developed a rash just about stocking top height on both legs and couldn't get rid of it. She had tried TCP and Valderma but to no avail; it wouldn't heal up. So she reluctantly went to see Dr Smith who had just recently moved to Cleator. He looked at the rash and asked her if she was married and she blushed and said, 'Yes Doctor,' wondering what he was going to say next. He was puzzled, then after looking down on the surgery floor and seeing what she had been wearing on her feet, looked up and said, 'It's nothing to worry about Mrs Greenlow, just cut two inches off the top of your wellies, and you'll be fine.'

I don't know how true this was, but again it's got to be seen in the context of humour before PC. Cruel though it may seem today, village life thrived on it in 1956.

The 'nobs' of Cleator were without a doubt the McCusker family. They owned the market garden and were one of the few families to employ any amount of local labour and still live within the village confines. Their business was labour intensive, and at one time they employed twenty men and boys. My father and uncles were amongst those employed as gardeners. One of my Dad's duties was to take the huge stock of fresh flowers to Corkickle Station in Whitehaven by horse and cart, to catch the half past four afternoon train to London, where the flowers would be taken to Covent Garden to be sold by auction at half past six the following morning.

Cleator people speak with great affection of the McCusker family because they were very fair-minded people and good employers, being deeply religious practising Catholics. The business was thriving and very profitable, allowing the ladies of the family to be just that, 'ladies'. They were quite elderly when I was a boy but they were so sweet to us all. They lived in the corner of Old Hall in two separate cottages. The family to the best of my knowledge, consisted of mother, son Matt and three sisters, May, Lily and Kitty.

I had occasion to call at Mrs McCusker's one wet October evening with a message in the form of a letter, given to my mother by Father McCann that morning coming out of ten past nine Mass. Mrs McCusker, seeing how wet I was, insisted on my going in and drying my hair and waiting for a break in the heavy showers before venturing back out.

She had the presence of an old Hollywood star and she was a bit like Queen Victoria with a perm, very fat and moved around seemingly on castors. The little front parlour was a cornucopia of chintz and lace doilies with a magnificent early Edwardian mahogany sideboard (I know this now because I've seen one similar in an antique shop in Kirby Lonsdale recently) decked with a silver candelabra as a centre piece, a statuette of a white pug dog on one side and a statue of St Martin in a glass dome on the other. Dotted between were ornately decorated silver picture-framed photographs of women in long dresses and Edwardian hats. There was also one of a horse-drawn trap and three very elegantly dressed women receiving a garland of flowers from a boy dressed in velvet breeches and a white blouson. A Grandfather clock with the words 'Whitehaven Clock Company' inscribed on the face stood stately next to the door leading to the kitchen, and a magnificent black slate fire grate with matching silver candlesticks and a silver carriage clock completed the picture.

This was grandeur on a small scale. Nothing too ostentatious but that was the McCuskers to a tee. Understated good taste except, it has to be said, for the appearance of two of the daughters.

The daughters, May and Lily had been brought up to play the piano and make polite conversation when entertaining the priests for afternoon tea. May had had her voice trained and in fact was a very accomplished singer. Nana Close said her rendition of 'Ava Maria' at the inaugural ceremony of the Cleator Grotto in 1927 was unforgettable. She had everybody in tears; you could have heard a pin drop. The congregation was spellbound. Afterwards, the Bishop said he had been to operas all over the world and she had the best voice he had ever heard. Alas, of late her appearance had degenerated into that of a mixture between Aunt Sally and Lily Savage. The ravages of time had forced her into a blonde wig and an over zealous rouge brush that did nothing to enforce the lovely warm charming and soft person which was the real May McCusker.

Matt McCusker had a very loud, deep, well-rounded voice. He sounded well educated and I fancy was quite opinionated and very vocal. I was standing at the bus stop outside of the *Three Tuns* one Saturday afternoon, waiting with Stephen and my mates for a bus to go to Egremont. We were going to see John Wayne at the matinee at the Castle Picture House and I could hear Matt's voice coming through the open window of the pub.

He seemed to be 'arguing the bit out' with somebody about the winner of the 2.30 at Newmarket, and it sounded as if he was nearly ready to fight somebody. Our Stephen heard him and said to me, 'Let me stand on your shoulders Sean, and I'll see if I can see what's going on through the window.'

Stephen scrambled on to my shoulders and just as he reached the open window, Jack Flemming, a regular of the *Tuns,* sitting next to the window, spotted Stephen and tried to grab him. Stephen drew back and lost his grip on the windowsill, slid into a sitting position on my

LITTLE IRELAND

shoulders and nearly 'necked' me. I couldn't take his weight and my knees buckled. Both of us landed on the pavement with a thump. My knees were grazed and Stephen hit his head and had a huge bump on it, and half the pub had come out to see if we were alright.

Jack Flemming was laughing his head off and Matt McCusker said, 'It's the Close twins isn't it, what the hell happened?'

Anyhow, just at that moment the bus arrived and we all jumped on, being no wiser as to who Matt was arguing with and Stephen and I feeling rather sorry for ourselves. Serves us right, you might be saying.

Sunday mornings were a treat when the McCusker family 'en masse' attended eleven o'clock Mass. They would arrive in their 1939 dark blue Daimler, driven by Matt, a very handsome, well-dressed portly man in his late fifties. Mrs McCusker would be helped out of the car by Matt, she wore a magnificent grey fox fur coat and a huge black hat with veil. She was so fat she could hardly walk. Then the sisters followed, or rather, floated out of the car looking like Bette Davis and Lauren Bacall at a distance. On closer scrutiny they were more like Bet Lynch and Rita Fairclough from Coronation Street, but they did cut a dash and made you feel you were going to a special occasion like the Cannes Film Festival or the BAFTA Awards, instead of High Mass at St Mary's with Father McCann never quite reaching the notes.

The McCusker's dressed up for every occasion, living in a glorious, glamorous world of their own.

None of the sisters nor brother Matt married, so the McCusker dynasty must have come to an end. Although, I think I can remember some talk of another sister who married an antique dealer from Penrith or somewhere. I never actually saw her, but maybe she had children and their lovely eccentric unworldly ways may have been passed on to this generation, and, God knows, we could do with them.

27
STREET LIFE

Cleator Village was teeming with life, both high and low life. It has a good cross section, from retired schoolteachers and doctors to poachers and 'tea-leaves'. From Jim Pettie the postman, who seems to rush about at a hundred-miles-an-hour and still have the 'crack' with everybody, to Mrs Madden from Old Hall, who practically crawls along and speaks to nobody.

The crack in Joe Graham's shop this morning is all about the beck being blown up last night. Ronnie Edgar and Jimmy Tate were noted for this. They put sticks of dynamite into the beck when the salmon were running and blew the beck up. The shock either killed the salmon or stunned them so they could easily be lifted out of the water.

No kidding. Apart from nearly blowing the iron bridge off its platform, the operation had been a complete success. Not only salmon were floating on the top, there were loads of smelt, some small trout and dozens of freshwater crabs and eels.

PC Jack Major and the two beck watchers were pacing up and down the bank like lunatics, looking for clues. No doubt Ronnie and Jimmy had been tried and convicted in Joe's shop already, but they're innocent until proven guilty by law, so it'll be interesting to see how it develops.

Getting back to blowing up the beck, I think the trick is to use detonators from the pit ammunition stores. The fish have no obvious signs of a violent death and they taste just as good as if they had been netted. They reckon that they can pick twenty or thirty salmon out of the beck with a single shot, at about o5.00 per fish, not bad for a night's work.

'But the police will catch them out and it'll be a gaol sentence for the boys if they do,' says Joe.

28
THE BANSHEE

Our next door neighbour-but-one is Barney McCourt. He lives in the end house and to be honest, I've only seen him once, or at least I think it was him.

Barney has loads of cats and was a bit of a character in his younger days, but he rarely ventures out nowadays. He was supposed to have had an old tomcat that howled all night, and the 'crack' goes that he was sick of people complaining about it.

One night some old Irishman on Prospect was dying and his family had been sent for. He was getting steadily worse when, all of a sudden, the family, who were sitting up with him, heard the cry of the banshee. They knew the old fellow was about to die, so they sent for the priest to give him the last rites. When the priest arrived he saw Barney's old tomcat and heard it crying, and explained to the family that it wasn't the banshee that they'd heard, but Barney's cat and that the old man wasn't dying at all.

The family complained to Barney the following day and he took the old cat in a Hessian sack weighed down with an old iron, and dropped it into the Lonny Beck. No banshees have been heard on Prospect since.

The windows of Barney's house have the curtains permanently drawn. They're practically hanging in shreds, but you never see him. I don't think he has any electricity in his house, and Bert Farren next door, says he hasn't any stairs either. He chopped them up to burn on the fire years ago. If he dies in bed they'll have a hell of a struggle to get his coffin in. Maybe they'll just drop him in the Lonny Beck in an old Hessian sack like his old tomcat.

It's all happening this week, first the Hen Beck getting blown up - no arrest as yet - and now Andrew Watson's pony is in trouble. Mind you it's been in trouble before, but this time it's in big trouble, at least Andrew is.

Andrew delivers the milk in Cleator with his pony and trap. He has two big milk drums on the back of the trap and he goes into everyone's back yard and fills the jugs they leave out for him. He has a milk ladle and he can fill almost six jugs with the one ladleful, so the pony follows him all the way up the backs when he calls it.

LITTLE IRELAND

However, this morning it didn't come for him, it was too busy biting the finger ends of Madge Womble's babby, Margaret, who was sitting in her pram in the back yard eating a crust of bread. Fanny Cricket said she heard the screams of the child from Prospect fronts where she was hanging out her washing.

Apparently Madge knocked hell out of the pony with the dolly legs and chased it before it actually ate the babbies hand off. It had a habit of nipping babbies that pony, but it's never bitten the fingers off before. Fanny Cricket says it bit her arse when she was bending down for a shovel of coal once.

Mam said the pony won't be allowed up Prospect backs again so Andrew will have to use his car in future, and poor Margaret Womble will never be able to give the 'V' sign with her right hand.

Life's a pig and then you die.

29
THE MONTH OF MAY

The month of May is dedicated to Our Blessed Lady in the Catholic Church. We sing special hymns everyday of the month dedicated to Our Lady and we have an altar to her in our classroom. Mr McCrickard is careful to point out to us that we do not actually adore Mary the Queen of the May, because we only adore God, but Mary is a very special saint. She was the earthly mother of God and we pray to her to pray to God for us.

The altar in our classroom has a statue of Our Lady, Our Lady of Lourdes and two vases. We bring fresh wild flowers throughout May, usually primroses and bluebells.

Hymn (1)

This is the image of our queen
Who reigns in bliss above
Of her who is the hope of man
Whom men and angels love
Most Holy Mary at thy feet
I'll bend a suppliant knee
On this thy own sweet month of May
Pray thou to god for me

Hymn (2)

Bring flowers of the rarest
Bring blossoms the fairest
From gardens and woodlands
And hillsides and dale.
Our full hearts are swelling
Our glad voices telling
The praise of the loveliest flower of the vale.
O Mary we crown thee with blossoms today
Queen of the angels and Queen of the May
O Mary we crown thee with blossoms today
Queen of the angels and Queen of the May

These happy joyous hymns fill my heart with love for everyone. To stand in front of this beautiful altar with its image of Mary, the spring flowers and warm sunlight drifting into our otherwise dull and miserable classroom can lift my spirit so high. May will always be the month of Our Lady for me.

I don't understand the concept of war. I don't know what hatred is and I have not yet experienced death. But I'm aware of the existence of these things.

So far, the nearest thing to unhappiness I have experienced is being locked in the classroom for an hour and a half with Mr McCrickard and thirty other children. This is mainly because I long to be running over the fields, jumping over the becks, finding birds' nests and doing a million things I *can't* do here.

Why do we need to know the names of all the capital cities of all the major countries of the world? I'm never going to go to any of them.

Then there's the 11+. I haven't 'a cat in hell's chance' of passing that, Mr McCrickard has as good as told me. The best I can hope for is a reasonable mark so that I'll be put in the 'A' form at St Cuthbert's. I'd rather be in the top stream at St Cuthbert's than the bottom stream in the Grammar School any day.

30
THE 11+ AND EXTRA CURRICULAR ACTIVITIES

The run up to the 11+ is upon us. Mr McCrickard has arranged evening classes with all the 11+ candidates; Tuesday and Thursday evenings, six o'clock to half past seven during the winter months. God I'm so depressed. I don't want to spend a single second longer than necessary in that bloody school. It's not fair.

Well fair or not, it was going to be, and for months we're slogging away doing fractions, long division, geometry, decimals, spelling, comprehension, problems and God knows what the hell else.

Mr McCrickard was a different person during the evening classes, he was far more relaxed and had time to come to everyone individually and explain in more detail. He even chain-smoked in the classroom. It seemed strange 'Old Crado' with a cigarette, it didn't suit him. He seemed to take such long draws, going really deep into his lungs, he even drew things on the board with the fag in his mouth. This is great - I quite fancy a fag myself, but I've never dared to try one.

The classroom felt somehow homely during the evening classes, everything seemed exaggerated and the whole place surrounded in quietness. The pot-bellied stove was white hot, not glowing red, and we sat around it in a circle instead of in rows like normal school time. The gaslights at the back of the classroom weren't lit so the focus of the room was around the fire and somehow around us.

We were made to feel important and for a while I began to realise I could be in with a chance with the 11+. 'Crado' had managed to impress the importance of a good education on me and I really was trying my best.

On the way home from the evening class, Eileen Flemming, Linda Williamson, Peter McDowell, Stephen and myself would wander down the styles, it was dark of course. This particular night the four of us (with Peter McDowell as lookout) climbed the fence into the field behind the high wall opposite Flosh Cottages for a snog. There was nothing unusual about this - just pre-pubescent curiosity, lip contact, very flat, how long can you kiss and hold your breath, it was a good laugh. Peter never took part and was always an unwilling lookout.

We were all snogging when suddenly a light was shining on us from the top of the wall. We all froze. A voice said, 'Come on you lot, show yourselves. What's going on down there?'

We all knew that what was going on would not be approved of by grownups and I recognised the voice, it was PC Jack Major. That bloody Peter McDowell had sloped off home and I wouldn't be surprised if he'd reported us to the police.

Well, we had two choices, we could give ourselves up and face Jack Major reporting us to our parents, or we could make a run for it and hope he doesn't recognise us. We all simultaneously opted for the latter and hoofed it down the style field, over the fence and into the park. I could feel the thumping of my heart and rush of adrenaline.

We were all determined not to be caught out. After all, we'd get a hiding from having the police call at our house and Mr McCrickard would give us the cane because Jack Major would be sure to report us to 'Old Crado'. Think of the explaining we would have to do. No, we had to escape.

Linda Williamson was crying, Stephen was saying 'You'd better be quiet Linda, or Jack Major will hear you.'

Jack Major shone the flashlight at us as we crossed the field and shouted at us to stop, but I don't suppose he was all that bothered about a group of kids snogging behind a wall. He didn't give chase, but shouted that he knew who we all were and he'd be going to tell our Dads.

We shit ourselves for about three days waiting for Jack Major, but he never arrived and we were far choosier whom we used for a lookout from then on. Peter McDowell had seen Jack Major, but was too terrified to give the alarm; he just froze on the spot. Mind you he had the decency to tell Jack Major he didn't know who we were, so we have to thank him for that.

This was a time of great change for our family and a time of even greater change for Stephen and myself because we were moving house shortly to Cleator Moor. Stephen and I would soon be going to a new school so we were excited and full of apprehension at the thought of going to a new school and everything that that would bring; new friends, new enemies, new teachers.

Better the devil you know than the devil you don't. Oh, maybe the teachers would be great, we'll see!

Cleator Moor is just a mile from Cleator, but at ten years of age it seems like a million miles and a whole different culture.

It's going to be strange at first.

31
I'M IN LOVE

I think I'm in love.

In fact, I'm *sure,* I'm in love.

I know I'm only ten years of age.

But I know how I feel.

We are staying at our beach bungalow at Nethertown for our annual summer holiday. We come here every August for about a month. My Dad, Uncle Eddie and Papa Heron built it years ago and all the family use it in turn. It's great.

It's a timber-framed building with insulation boards on the inside and flat asbestos sheets on the outside with a corrugated asbestos roof. It's painted maroon and has a long verandah, the full length of the front. This is where all the aunties, uncles and friends who come to visit us, sit and have the 'crack' and endless cups of tea and bottles of beer in the long summer evenings.

Looking back, it would seem a strange tradition to go on holiday and have all your friends and relations visit you at weekends, but Nethertown is only eight miles from Cleator, so people seemed to come and go all the time. Mealtimes are no problem because everybody mucks in, the relatives bringing loads of food with them, and it all seems to happen without any fuss.

The inside of the bungalow consists of kitchen with Calor Gas stove and running water, a living-room with two windows and a front door opening out onto the verandah, and a huge range with an oven and a chimney breast and Calor Gas lighting. Three bedrooms, one double room on its own and two double rooms leading one onto the other. And there's an outside loo.

There's a big old caravan in the garden which is mainly used for all the lads to sleep in when there's a big family party staying. That's when we have the best time of all.

The caravan's a bit wrecked, but we only use it to sleep in. There's often ten of us sleeping in it at once, but there's plenty of beds. In fact it's all beds and 'shakey-downs'.

Nana and Papa come down at the weekends, but Papa won't stay the night. He says he likes his own bed.

LITTLE IRELAND

The bungalow is called 'High View' because its perched on the top of the cliff, overlooking the breakwater and you can see Scotland and the Isle of Man. It's in its own little hollow and Dad keeps the grass cut all around the bungalow so we can play cricket, rounders and tennis, and there's lots of room.

Next to us up the hill is *'Borneo'*, its owned by the Coile family. Their lads Gordon and Alan, are about our age so they often come to play cricket with us. A couple of nights ago we had a bonfire and old Mr Coiles brought his accordion out and played loads of old tunes. Mam and Auntie Lily and Winnie thought it was great.

Actually, the evening's entertainment was brought to a sudden halt when our Stephen had an accident. We'd been playing a game of gymnastics with our cousin Shaun Devoy and Raymond Graham. We were doing handstands and somersaults and half-arm flips over an old car seat when Stephen somehow lost his footing. He fell over the car seat and landed on his arm. You would have thought he'd been murdered, the cries out of him.

Everybody rushed over to see what was wrong and old Mr Coiles said, 'I think he's broken his arm.'

He took Stephen, Auntie Winnie and Mam in his car to Whitehaven Hospital. We were all crying because he seemed to be in such a lot of pain. Stephen had to stay in overnight. They let him out the following morning, complete with plaster cast and a sling. What a fuss everybody made of him. 'No more gymnastics this summer', Mam said.

I think Shaun Devoy's getting the blame for not supervising properly. It wasn't his fault, Stephen's always having accidents.

The little strip of land between the railway line and the seashore has about ten bungalows and as many static caravans on it. Ours is in the best place because it's the last plot and there's only the breakwater and the railway line next to us.

It's very quiet.

32
BRICEY FINN

Bricey Finn from Main Street, Cleator, had a bungalow on the top of the hill just up from us. It had been sold recently because Bricey was killed last winter. Cleator people are still getting over the shock of her death. All I know is she was shot dead by her boyfriend, Tony Steele, who had one of the farms in Nethertown village.

We heard he shot her in the barn at Nethertown then turned the gun on himself. What a terrible thing to do. Actually Mam says he shot her in the house they had been sharing in Frizington. She had left him just before Christmas and gone back to her husband at Cleator. When she went back to the house at Frizington for her clothes he was waiting for her. He shot her and then turned the gun on himself. The crack was being mixed up with Tony's father who was supposed to have hanged himself in the barn at Nethertown.

Bricey was a lovely woman. We lived back-to-back with her at Cleator and used to see her all the time. She always said hello to us and gave us sweets. They were both married to other people, so maybe that was something to do with it.

We always played in Tony's barn when it is raining. He doesn't really mind as long as we don't disturb the bales too much. We got a long piece of rope from one of the beams and we use it to swing from, or at least we used to. I'm never going into that barn again. 'There must be blood splattered on all the walls', our Barry says.

Last summer when we were playing in the barn, which was nearly full of hay, so we couldn't use the swing, my mate Tom Osowski was missing for over an hour. We thought he'd gone home because he was always hitting his head on the beams at the top of the hay bales. We christened him 'Beam Boy'. Nobody knew where he had gone so we assumed he had just sneaked off to lick his wounds.

After we all left the barn and went back to the bungalow I went to see if he was alright. He was staying in Bricey's caravan next to her bungalow. His Mam said he hadn't got back yet, so a search party was set up to find him. He was eventually found in the barn. He had slipped between a gap in the bales and had gone down to the barn floor, about eighteen feet from where he'd been standing on the top of the hay bales. He said he'd been shouting for us for ages, but we couldn't hear him. Mam said he could have suffocated, and if we went near that barn again she'd kill us. She needn't have worried because wild horses couldn't drag us into that barn after what happened to poor Bricey.

33
LINDA STRICKLAND

To get back to my love life.. I met Linda Strickland when we were out on the rocks looking for crabs. She was with her mate who was staying with them in the McNally's bungalow, which was not far from ours. She had found a crab under some rocks and was frightened to lift it up. So I picked it up by the claws and plopped it into her bucket. She was chuffed to bits and we all got talking, Raymond Graham, Linda and her mate and me. We talked for ages.

Linda was a bit older than I was and I thought she was the loveliest thing I had ever seen. She looked just like Helen Shapiro. She told me she had lived most of her life in Whitehaven, but had moved with her family to Cleator Moor this spring and they knew the McNallys. That's how they were here in Nethertown.

She said she had seen me a few times when she was passing us on the Nethertown road in her Dad's car and had waved at me, but I never waved back. I did think I'd seen someone waving one afternoon on that road, but I wasn't sure so I didn't wave back.

I asked her, 'Has your Dad got a green three-wheeler car?' and she said, 'Yes.'

So I had seen her, but I couldn't understand why she waved at me.

She said she fancied me. I was made up. We arranged to meet later that night by the air-raid shelter on the hill down to the far beach and my heart was racing like mad. I knew I must be in love.

Raymond Graham didn't fancy her mate, but he reluctantly agreed to come with me after we had our dinner. I told Mam and Auntie Lily, Raymond's mother, we were going for a walk and they said, 'Mind you're back before it gets dark.'

Well, you know how it is, time flies when you're enjoying yourself. We walked along the sand hand-in-hand, hoping no-one would see us and it was starting to get dark so we set off to get back.

By the time we got to the air-raid shelter it was actually dark and we all knew we'd be in trouble. Panic set in and I said, 'Come on we'd better get back before they send someone to find us'.

Just at that moment, Linda grabbed me and put her lips on mine and kept them there for ages. I was quite shocked and was pleased when she finally let go. She said, 'Let's meet tomorrow afternoon and go for another walk,' and I agreed.

Raymond said, 'You can go on your own, I'm not coming. I'm going fishing with Uncle Jay.'

Linda ran in to be greeted by her father, who we could see from the road was not very pleased, and he glared at us as we passed by. Mam and Auntie Lily were not too bothered, they said we were late and to be back before this time tomorrow night or we wouldn't be allowed out after dinner again.

I couldn't sleep for thinking about that kiss, it seemed to last forever. Mostly though I liked her. She talked about all sorts of different things and she was interesting and had a nice face and nice lips. Yes, very nice lips. I had snogged before with Linda Williamson, but that was just a game - this was different, I was definitely smitten. I just couldn't get to sleep.

Finally I must have slept. In fact it was half past ten and Mam was waking me up. She said, 'Come on, you've slept long enough. The lads are all going down to the breakwater for a swim. Auntie Lily and I will bring you all some sandwiches later. Your dad's going to set the line when the tide goes out so you'll need to help him get some bait.'

Bait! 'Sod that,' I thought, 'I'm meeting Linda this afternoon.'

The swim was alright, a bit cold but not bad. I wasn't in the mood. Mam and Auntie Lily came as promised, with armfuls of sandwiches and crisps and pop, but nothing could lift my spirits. I wanted to see Linda.

I wandered down the beach to the lagoon where a porpoise had been washed up. It had been alive for hours struggling in the shallow lagoon but couldn't survive. That was three weeks ago. It must have been ill before it landed in the lagoon. It attracted a big crowd. We had watched it from the cliff until it got dark and the next morning it was washed up on the stones as dead as a nit. It was huge.

The crows and seagulls had picked its eyes out and it was lying in a swarm of flies, you could smell it half a mile away. It was all bloated up and Shaun Devoy said, 'It's filling up with gas and it will explode blood and guts all over the beach when it finally pops.' I had to hold my nose, but my frame of mind drove me on with a morbid curiosity.

What a bloody mess! The day it was washed up, Barry and Stephen climbed up on its back, and someone took a photograph of them. We were expecting to see the photograph any day. I didn't fancy climbing on its back. That's no way to treat a dead animal, especially one as big as that.

I climbed the steep steps that had been cut out of the sods on the cliff. It struck me that whoever had cut these steps out must have spent weeks doing it. Who could be bothered to put such effort into making steps down the cliff when there's a path further down?

Then I remembered the reason for the steps. They were used every night by the people who used the caravans; they didn't have cesspits so they had to empty the dry toilets on the rocks every night after dark. They had to go as far out as they could so that the tide would take it away. This is where we picked the covens. Dad said that's why they're so good at that point; the sewage makes them grow, yeuk!

Mind you I love the covens, we collect them and Dad steeps them in salt water overnight to clean them, he then washes them out four or five times and boils them for an hour. They're lovely with vinegar and a slice of bread and butter.

Dad's got us well trained. Every time we go beachcombing, and that's every day, at some time in the day we take a plastic bag with us and collect driftwood. Just small bits of wave-battered wood, bits of wooden crates thrown overboard from the fishing boats or maybe from the Marchon trader going back and forth to Tangiers. A bagful makes a lovely fire later on when the temperature drops.

I found my excuse to go back to the bungalow just after one o'clock because Auntie Lily had run out of cigarettes and I had said I'd go to the shop and get some for her. She gave me the bungalow key and told me where to find her purse. I was off like a shot, up the steep path by the railway line to the bungalow, got the money and very furtively passed Linda's bungalow.

The three-wheeler car wasn't there and there was no sign of anyone. The whole place was deserted. I just remembered we hadn't made any definite arrangements, just we'll meet tomorrow afternoon. What a prat I am! Now where can she be?

Anyhow, I go to the shop and Mr Wallace wraps the cigarettes in a brown paper bag and says, 'Don't let anybody see you with them.'

I'm now back at the air raid shelter pacing up and down like a caged animal. The rest of the day was hell. I took Auntie Lily her fags and brooded around, refusing to play with anybody or go and set the

LITTLE IRELAND

line with Dad. No, I wanted to be on my own. Mam couldn't understand it, she said to Auntie Lily, 'He must be sickening for something because Sean's never like this.'

I can't describe my anguish. Linda must think I've stood her up and she'll never speak to me again.

The day went by somehow, although I don't know how I spent it. We went back to the bungalow and eventually had some dinner. Raymond wanted to play cards so I played a few hands of Whist but soon got sick of that. Then Auntie Lily, who was sweeping the floor at the time, asked, 'What's this under the doormat Eileen? Someone must have put it through the letterbox.'

Mam said, 'It's a letter with our Sean's name on it.'

So I walked up to Lily and said, 'Lets see Auntie Lily.'

She wasn't for giving it to me at first, she said, 'Should I open it for you and see who its from?' and I said, 'No, its for me'.

So she passed it to me. I knew it was from Linda. I took it from her and everybody was gawping at me, so I went into the bedroom.

Dear Sean

I'm sorry about this afternoon, my Dad wouldn't let me out after last night so we had to go to the Ratty instead. I haven't to see you anymore my Dad says and he's keeping an eye on me for the rest of the week. We're going home the day after tomorrow and I'm desperate to see you. I will never forget our kiss by the air raid shelter, I love you.

Please try and find a way to see me before we go home,

All my love, Linda.

My heart was racing and I felt sick. What could I do? She must be pining away and I've got to see her. In my state of shock I put the letter down and went back in the living room where everybody was waiting to hear my news.

Mam said, 'Well, who was the letter from?'

In my attempts to protect my embarrassment I said, 'Nobody, there was nothing in the envelope.'

Auntie Lily said with a laugh in her voice, 'You wee liar, its from a girlfriend, isn't it?'

She ran into the bedroom and came out with the letter. I was beside myself. I ran across the room and tried to grab the letter, which by this time she was reading out loud. The words were out: '*I will never forget our kiss by the air raid shelter*' Auntie Lily read amidst howls of laughter from Auntie Winnie, who had just arrived and Mam was not amused, 'Now you can cut this out, lasses at your age, who is she?'

I couldn't stand it any more, I was mortified. I felt as ashamed as if I'd been found out doing something terrible. I was embarrassed at everybody laughing at me, it wasn't a joke, I just wanted to die.

I ran into the bedroom and hid my face under the pillow, I stayed there for ages until Mam came in. She sat beside me on the bed and put her hand on my back. I didn't know what to expect. She was very calm, but I wasn't. She said, 'Listen son, you're too young to be kissing lasses. That Linda Strickland is 13, she's too old for you anyhow. Now you leave well alone.'

I turned round and was crying. I sat up on the bed and said, 'Auntie Lily and Auntie Winnie were laughing at me Mam, and they shouldn't laugh, its not funny, I can't face them.'

Mam said, 'You know our Lily and Winnie like a good laugh, but I'll tell them not to go on about it, so don't worry about them. Come back through and I'll give you a glass of lemonade and a biscuit. Come on lad, you'll have to face them sooner or later.'

Auntie Winnie and Lily had been told to button it, but I could feel the forced quietness in the room for the rest of the night. I was glad when all the lads retired to the caravan to bed.

The weather broke during the night and I could hear the heavy raindrops on the caravan tin roof. It sounded quite comforting to be warm, dry and out of the storm.

The following morning Mam said it was forecast heavy rain for the next few days. She was going to the farm and to the shop to stock up while the rain had eased off and asked if anyone wanted to go with her. Barry, Stephen, Raymond and Shaun had been doing jigsaws, but I needed to stretch my legs so I said I would go and help her carry the milk.

On our way down the hill past the railway bridge we had to cut into the side because a car was going past, and when I looked it was the Stricklands' three-wheeler. They never even papped at us and Linda didn't even turn round.

Mam said that she'd heard they'd decided to go home a day early because of the weather, 'So it's maybe just as well lad.'

I said 'I suppose so.'

I never clapped eyes on Linda Strickland from that day to this, but she will always have a special place in my heart.

34
ESCAPE FROM AUSCHWITZ

The wind's picked up and the rain's coming down. Nethertown, with its shanty town bungalows and deserted army camp air raid shelters and lookout bunkers, resembles a war zone, so not surprisingly our boyish minds turn to war games.

Just opposite our bungalow on the cliff edge, are a group of sand dunes, partly grassed over. Two of the dunes are in the form of round hollows, about six feet wide and about four feet deep. One oval in shape and the other almost round, about four feet apart. We use them for sun bathing when the weather is hot, because you're out of the winds that sweep up the cliff top.

We can play with our toy soldiers and bury makeshift land mines in the soft sand hoping to blow up unsuspecting Germans, who pass by on reconnaissance missions. Today, sunbathing in the soft sand and looking up at the cotton wool clouds is just a distant memory, but we're under Mam's feet in the bungalow, so Barry suggests we borrow an old tarpaulin from under the caravan and make a camp in the sand dunes.

The tarpaulin is at least twenty feet long and ten feet wide and will easily go over both sand dunes. All we need is a couple of clothes props and a load of rocks from the shore and we can bivouac to our hearts' content. After we have erected the tarpaulin (it takes ages because of the high winds) we're able to shelter from the rain, and although the tarpaulin is being battered by the storm, and at least one of our battalion is fully occupied constantly replacing the rock and securing the tarpaulin, the rest of us can engage in war games.

The soft sand is very easy to dig and Shaun Devoy suggests we dig a tunnel from one dune to the other, pretending we're escaping from a prisoner of war camp, so we need timbers as props to form our tunnel, some four feet long.

I'm sent out to search for materials and return some ten minutes later with an armful of fencing palings. Dad has been using them to make a fence behind the bungalow. They had originally been about ten feet long, but loads of short off-cuts had been stored in the shed to cut up for firewood, these would be ideal. So after much praise from Commander Devoy, and the promise of a commendation after the war for my efforts, we set about digging the tunnel.

That was the thing about our cousin Shaun Devoy, he was three years older than myself and Stephen, and a natural leader, who knew how to praise his men to get the best results from them.

We all worked happily away for the rest of the morning, digging the sand out with our bare hands. After we were a foot or so into the bank we forced a short piece of timber in place to form the start of the ceiling for our tunnel. Mam was shouting to us to come for our dinner so Shaun Devoy went over to see if we could have our chips and beans in the camp.

Inside the camp, which was barely light, just shafts of light filtering in from the gaps in the tarpaulin where we had formed a doorway, we could stand up and walk around and smell the salty damp sand we'd been digging in. This gave us enormous appetites and the chips and beans went down a treat.

By 4.30 the tunnel was almost complete and we'd used up all the timber off-cuts so some improvisation was needed to complete the last nine inches or so of our tunnel. We cut into the bank at an angle to the other dune, to make the tunnel more interesting, so that by the time we'd made a turn in the tunnel to get back on course, it was about six feet long. Raymond suggested we take a couple of roof struts from just inside the tunnel to complete the last piece of ceiling. So, he and Stephen set about removing two of the centre struts. That's when the catastrophe happened.

Stephen was right at the end of the tunnel waiting to be handed the roof strut from Raymond when the roof collapsed. Raymond managed to push himself out backwards on his belly, but Stephen was trapped. He had about 2' 6" of wet sand on top of him and the tunnel had collapsed about two feet from the entrance.

There was turmoil in the camp. We couldn't hear a sound from Stephen and we knew we had to act quickly. Barry, Shaun Devoy and I dived over the sand into the far sand dune and started digging frantically with our bare hands. Raymond climbed onto the top of the sand dune and started to dig from above.

We had estimated the tunnel to be about six feet long from end to end, but because of the angle, we weren't exactly sure where it would come out, so we all dug next to each other to hedge our bets.

Within minutes, Barry had unearthed Stephen's hand and within another half a minute we had him out of the tunnel. His mouth, nose and eyes were full of sand and he was absolutely panic stricken, shouting, 'I'm going to die, I'm going to die.'

Well, of course, he wasn't going to die, he was breathing and yelling, but Stephen did tend to panic at the best of times, though he did have cause for concern this time, it has to be said.

Shaun Devoy swore us to secrecy over this with the threat of a court martial or even a firing squad if we breathed a word to anybody. After all, this was wartime and we were engaged in active service. We had planned to camp out all night if Mam and Auntie Winnie would let us, Shaun Devoy was convinced they'd be alright about it, but after our Stephen's near death experience none of us mentioned camping out that night. We were all secretly glad he was alright and we put the incident behind us and wrote it off as a bad experience.

The following morning we took the tarpaulin down and folded it up and pushed it back under the caravan and then threw the stones down the cliff to the shore. This was done almost ritualistically, making sure nothing was left visible of our camp.

I think subconsciously we were eradicating the whole experience from our minds by meticulously removing any visible evidence of the camp, except of course, the wide hollow joining the dunes together left by the collapsed tunnel, which would be a permanent memorial of our folly.

Stephen's dance with death really frightened us all. Well, as all childhood experiences pale into insignificance with the passing of a day and a new experience, so would this, in fact our new best friend was to fill our last week at Nethertown with even more memorable experiences.

35
F****** JOHN

His name was John Gray, he came from Lockerbie in Scotland and was for all the world a latter day Rab C Nesbitt. I had real trouble understanding a word he said, and in fact some of the words he used I'd truly never heard before. He was like a character from the *'Beano'*. He wore boots with steel corkers, grey knee-length socks, short brown corduroy pants, a round neck Arran jumper and a maroon corduroy bomber jacket with a woolly hat. This was Nethertown in late August. He looked fit for a trek on the Mull of Kintyre in February half-term holidays.

He introduced Stephen and me to more four-letter words than you could shake a stick at. We christened him F****** John. Work that one out!

Even now, I think that four-letter words sound more threatening with a Scottish accent, so to be introduced to the Anglo-Saxon expletives by a Scot was terrifying at ten years of age. Let's be fair, even a foreigner would know what was being said if John Grey told him to 'F*** off', which he tended to do to most people.

How do we know swear words are swear words when we first hear them? Well, we just do. We instinctively know not to say them to anybody over fifteen years of age.

The nearest thing to a swear word I'd ever heard prior to my John Gray experience, was overhearing Auntie Winnie relaying a conversation she had just had with Uncle Eddie to Mam, when she told him to 'Kiss my arse, Eddie.'

I was shocked at that, so John Gray was about to take me down the rocky road to hell with his swear words.

After about an hour with John I felt a serious need for confession. I felt my modesty injured. His ability to use a different word for the female private parts every ten seconds of every conversation was phenomenal. I know he was evil, but I could not resist him and neither could our Stephen. Mam said, 'There's something about that lad I don't like, why do you need to play with him when you've got each other?'

Well, she may well ask, but John Gray courted danger and rubbed shoulders with the obscene and we were drawn to him like 'moths to a candle'.

After the initial shock of F****** John, he was very entertaining. He didn't seem to feel pain and he was so ugly. He had a big brown mole on his cheek, the greyest skin I have ever seen, buck teeth and a short tongue. Can you wonder at my mother being suspicious of him?

Truly, I don't know how we understood a word he said. You know, some of the Scottish border accents are harder to understand than the Highland accents. Well, his certainly was, ye ken.

The three of us spent the next five days up and down the coast like some gang of marauding bandits. We broke into a caravan at Caulderton, well, actually, it wasn't locked, but we shouldn't have been there. John wanted to trash it, but Stephen and I just managed to stop him before he did any damage. We went on walkabout to Braystones and captured a rowing boat on the tarn. John wanted to sink it, but again we managed to restrain him.

One day we walked almost to Sellafield and found a crate of Pall Mall cigarettes which had been washed up on the beach, partly covered in sand. They must have been thrown overboard by pirates who had been scooped by customs' boats patrolling the Solway Firth. Well, they could have been! How else could they have landed on the beach? No-one throws a crate of cigarettes overboard by accident.

This was real high drama. We took about ten packets each to the bungalow for Dad, but they had been in the sea and were totally unsmokable, Dad said. They must have been bad for Dad to refuse them; he would smoke horseshit, if there was nothing else.

John was too dangerous for us. He was in a different league and we certainly couldn't keep up with him, nor did we want to really, although the excitement of being with this crook for a few days was fantastic.

He told us he'd been in trouble with the police in Lockerbie for breaking into a billiard hall. So he was well on the way to a life of crime, he just couldn't help himself.

On the way home from finding the Pall Malls, John threw a brick through Minnie Copleton's caravan window and ran like hell, leaving Stephen and me to face the music. We ran like hell too, because we didn't want to have to split on him. Five days of overkill with John Gray had absolutely exhausted Stephen and me and on that last

LITTLE IRELAND

Saturday morning we refused to go for a walk to pick mushrooms with him knowing full well we'd be persuaded to rob Tony Steele's hen hut or nick fags from Mr Wallace's shop.

The morning was warm and a bit damp. We helped Mam and Dad to load Papa Heron's car with cases and pillowcases of washing and piles of bedding and boxes of toys and fishing tackle.

Four weeks is a long time in the life of a ten-year-old and we had so much to tell our mates when we got back to Cleator. It was nice going back home to the familiar things and the crack on the backs. But we'd had a great summer holiday and part of me wanted to stay.

I've only been able to tell you a small part of what we did on holiday in Nethertown, we did so much more. We caught butterflies and grasshoppers and dragonflies in bottles. We went train spotting - you know if you put a halfpenny on the railway line and let a train ride over it, it ends up as big as a penny, but the chuddy machine at the Tow Bar shop won't accept them!

We went rabbiting, mushrooming and beachcombing. We sneaked out of the bungalow at midnight once and went skinny-dipping in the tide, we even made a garden with wild flowers along the side of the bungalow and watered them every day. Every single minute had been an adventure and I'm ready for a rest.

But we'll be back next Easter to air the beds and take the shutters off the windows and Papa Heron will say as we approach the railway bridge, 'See who can see the sea first lads'. And it will all start again. Please God.

36
THE OLD SILVER ROVER

When we got back from Nethertown that year things felt different. The ominous task for Mam and Dad of packing things ready for our house move seemed to weigh heavily on us children.

We were very excited about our move to Cleator Moor. In fact Aunty Mary and her family had already left Cleator and Uncle Henry and his family and Aunty Winnie and her family were moving shortly after us. So, soon our happy united families were going to be split up. Things would probably never be the same again and I sensed this profoundly.

My last memory of Cleator village was the old silver Rover. It was parked up on the waste ground at the end of Prospect Row, behind Church Went. We'd noticed it off and on for a few days; the last few days of our summer holidays from school just after we returned to Cleator after our stay at Nethertown. The lads on the backs were playing on it, jumping on and off its tail boards and standing on its chrome bumpers. It was a faded silver grey colour and it had a huge covered spare wheel attached to the boot. It had dark blue leather upholstery and a faded roller blind on the back window.

No-one seemed to know who it belonged to. Very few people in Cleator had cars at that time, so there was much speculation as to who owned it.

The day we actually moved was a Saturday, the last weekend of the summer holidays, September 1959. We were still in the dark about the silver Rover until Dad said, 'Come on lads lets get some of the clothes into the car before the removal men come for the furniture'.

This was typical of Dad. He'd kept the car a secret to highlight the excitement for us on our last day at Prospect Row, as if we needed any more excitement than moving house!

We were all bowled over, not only were we moving house today, but we had a new car to take with us to our new life at Cleator Moor. We could hardly take it all in.

Dad used to do some gardening for Dr Fitch and when the doctor was drowned off St Bees Head in his fishing boat, Dad did some driving for his wife in the old silver Rover. Eventually she decided to

LITTLE IRELAND

leave Cleator and return to relatives in the south of England, so she offered Dad first refusal of the Rover. He'd paid her the princely sum of thirty pounds for it, and it was magnificent.

It had a walnut dashboard and the blue leather upholstery smelled of polish. The front seats had a flap on the back of them which folded down to make extra seats and the windows were smoked glass. It was like something from a war film. The roller blind on the back window was operated by a cord attached to a pulley system with the handle in the front of the car. Dad cranked the engine with a handle the first time he started it, because it hadn't been started for several days, but after that the ignition key did the job.

We were leaving Cleator village in style with a whole new life at Cleator Moor to go to and a car to impress all our new neighbours with. It all seemed so unreal. We were like The Larkins from the Darling Buds of May!

The late-August sun shone through the little sash windows of our old empty house at Prospect Row and a million memories flooded my head. It had been a happy house for us.

Mam and Dad showed no obvious signs of emotion. They would probably be back again to give the floorboards a final sweep and say their farewells, but this was to be my last glimpse of the only home I'd known.

The dark green paint on the ancient tongue-and-grooved partition wall in the kitchen was peppered with small nail holes where a 1959 calendar had hung and numerous others had hung before it, and the dark brown shiny slopstone and wooden draining-board in the corner of the room were empty for the first time in my memory. In fact, the only thing that remained in the house was the bench Dad had made so we could all sit round the kitchen table together to have our meals. I don't know why that was being left and I didn't ask. I just wanted to go now.

We had seen the house on the new housing estate at Cleator Moor once before, but only from the outside. 12 Croasdale Place was the address. It all looked so new. The paths and roads were perfectly smooth tarmac and the round kerbstones of the cul-de-sac were a perfect circle; it looked like an architect's model.

The front doors were all different colours - dark blues, deep oranges, vivid reds and fluorescent greens. The windows were painted pure white and the gardens were newly top soiled and open plan. It was a complete contrast to what we'd left behind and I felt an overwhelming sense of excitement.

Mam and Dad laughed the whole day. I think this is the happiest day of my life.

The house inside smelled of Parazone and new paint. Every room was painted magnolia and it sounded hollow and very noisy, but starkly welcoming. Mam and Dad had been given the key a couple of days earlier and had fitted oilcloth in the bedrooms and bathroom. The kitchen and living-room had Bakelite floor tiles fitted by the council; wood grain colour in the living-room and grey speckled in the kitchen.

The kitchen had a cream anodised sink supported on metal legs (no sink unit or work tops), a gas boiler for boiling cloths had been provided by the council and our own gas cooker from Cleator stood in one corner looking rather lost.

A new Formica table and sideboard in mock oak with matching chairs completed the furnishings. Worktops would have to be added later. There was also an outhouse and coalhouse next to the kitchen leading to the back door. The living room had a peculiar cream coloured fire grate with a back boiler and an all night burner. This was the full extent of the heating system.

The three bedrooms were small; in fact one was just a glorified box room, but we would have to use it as a bedroom for Margaret. Barry, Stephen and myself had the biggest room in the front of the house with a double bed and a single bed in it. This left hardly any room for the wardrobe and dressing table and leaving only a small gap for access to the beds. We seemed to have left a much bigger house at Cleator, but at least we had a bathroom and smooth walls.

Mam had made a conscious effort to hurl herself into the 1960s with her new furniture for the living room. The new three-piece suite was black moquette with dark blue cushions on spindly black legs, furnished with an array of scatter cushions in yellow, bright red and turquoise. There was a standard lamp with an orange shade, a picture of Don Quixote in a gilt frame above the fire grate, and a pair of zigzag designed white, fibreglass curtains at the windows. It looked really chic.

Minimalist was the latest thing; gone was the clutter. No more bordered wallpapers with flowers, no more heavy oak tables or hookey mats and china cabinets, antimacassars and doilies. The

LITTLE IRELAND

television was placed on a low coffee table with thin black legs. Soon the fitted carpets would arrive and the walls would be painted dove grey with Wedgwood blue doors. The war years had gone forever. We had moved house and re-invented ourselves.

This was the time to move on. The full employment of the late 50s had left us with a feeling of security. Optimism had turned into aspiration. The world was our oyster. The likes of us could suddenly do anything. People from our estate were going to the Grammar School and onto college and university, trade apprenticeships abounded. The local factories were crying out for labour and married women were taking part-time jobs. Farm work and the pits were no longer the only options.

Sellafield was in full swing and ordinary people were buying cars for the first time and all of this just as we arrived at Cleator Moor. We thought we were some bugger. And why not?

A hymn

Oh Mother I could weep for mirth
Joy fills my heart so fast
My soul today is heaven on earth
Oh could the transport last
I think of thee and what thou art
Thy majesty confess
And I keep singing in my heart
Immaculate Immaculate